Dan Kiley
Landscapes

Dan Kiley Landscapes

THE POETRY OF SPACE

Edited by
Reuben M. Rainey + Marc Treib

UNIVERSITY OF VIRGINIA
SCHOOL OF ARCHITECTURE

WILLIAM STOUT
PUBLISHERS
RICHMOND, CALIFORNIA

© School of Architecture,
University of Virginia,
publication, introduction, and panel discussion;
essays copyright by individual authors.
All rights reserved.

ISBN 978-0-9795508-7-4
Library of Congress Control Number 2009924274

Designed by Marc Treib

Figures credited to the Office of Dan Kiley
are provided courtesy of Marc Treib

Published by
William Stout Publishers
1326–1328 South 51st Street
Richmond, California 94804

www.stoutpublishers.com

Printed in China

Frontispiece:
**DAN KILEY,
LANDSCAPE ARCHITECT;
ROCHE AND DINKELOO,
ARCHITECTS;
OAKLAND MUSEUM,
OAKLAND, CALIFORNIA,
1969.**
/ MARC TREIB /

Dan Kiley:
An Introduction

Reuben M. Rainey
Marc Treib

Daniel Urban Kiley (1912–2004) was one of the most gifted and productive American landscape architects of the twentieth century. Born into a blue-collar family in Boston, he embodied throughout his life the sharp wit, lack of pretension, exuberant spirit, and no-nonsense directness of his Irish heritage. As a good New Englander he could be argumentative and stubborn, but his opinions were almost always accompanied by a twinkle of the eye. The architect Harry Wolf echoed the thoughts of many in his profession when he spoke of Kiley's "prodigious talent" as well as the "presence of his spirit" as a "special elixir" for those collaborating with him.[1]

After an apprenticeship in the Boston office of Warren Manning, in the mid-1930s Kiley passed through the landscape architecture program at Harvard University as a special student, a status granted because he had no formal education beyond high school. Although he never earned a degree while at Harvard, he met and befriended the other two members of the trio that would profoundly shape the practice of American landscape architecture in the post-war years: Garrett Eckbo and James Rose. In 1940 Kiley collaborated with these former classmates— although Rose and Eckbo did most of the writing—to produce three classic articles that boldly reformulated the scope and practice of landscape architecture in succeeding years.[2]

In mature professional life Kiley worked hard and played hard, producing an astounding number of significant projects. Many of these designs were collaborative efforts with the outstanding architects of his time: Louis Kahn, Eero Saarinen, I. M. Pei, Kevin Roche, Edward Larabee Barnes, Richard Meier, and Harry Wolf among others. These collaborative projects number among the most significant in mid- to late-twentieth-century America: the Jefferson National Expansion Memorial, the Miller

DAN KILEY,
LANDSCAPE ARCHITECT;
SKIDMORE OWINGS MERRILL,
ARCHITECTS;
UNITED STATES
AIR FORCE ACADEMY,
COLORADO SPRINGS,
COLORADO, 1957–1968.

/ MARC TREIB /

garden, Dulles Airport, the United States Air Force Academy, the East Wing of the National Gallery, Rockefeller University, the Dallas Art Museum, the Oakland Museum, Fountain Place in Dallas, Texas, and the Lincoln Center for the Performing Arts.

In the midst of productivity worthy of a Frederick Law Olmsted, Kiley found time to relish life through such pursuits as exhilarating ski runs on the Vermont slopes, quick spins in his Morgan, brisk sails on Lake Champlain, six-a.m. rounds of golf with his staff, or gourmet meals graced with a fine vintage. An ardent reader with the typically broad interests of an autodidact, he steeped himself especially in the works of Ralph Waldo Emerson, Henry David Thoreau, Lewis Mumford, and Carl Jung, upon which he called on occasion to buttress his own approach to design.

This introduction is not the place to analyze Kiley's landscape architecture in detail; we leave that to the contributors to this volume. However, it is important to emphasize that Kiley's designs are not static vignettes for the eye alone but instead dynamic, unfolding, multi-sensual spatial sequences of discovery that he referred to as "the poetry of space"—acknowledging the role of art in his practice. Photographs may capture some qualities of the Kiley landscapes but they hardly do justice to their nuanced richness.

Kiley embraced a humanistic point of view. For him it was not "man *and* nature" or "man *with* nature," but "man *is* nature." He understood ecology and its influence on design, but never attempted to replicate the literal appearance of nature in his landscapes. Instead, he sought the principles

of order and the processes behind natural systems and transformed them—often through the "classical" landscape elements of the bosque, the parterre, the terrace, the allée, and the axis—to create engaging, at times delightful, settings for human activity. He saw no discrepancy between the rigor of Euclidian geometry and the complex reality of nature: "man *is* nature."

Sadly, Kiley left us few written accounts of his approach to design.[3] In the early 1970s, when his reputation as one of the nation's leading landscape architects had been assured, a publisher approached him about writing a book on his philosophy of design. Somehow that initiative fell through. In recounting this episode in 1982, he remarked with typical wit and candor, "I'm glad I never wrote anything, because it would have been as dumb as hell... to start to write before you have done anything is very dangerous."[4] Following his own advice with the rigor of an Olympic athlete, Kiley periodically produced only a few short essays and waited until his eighty-seventh year to co-author a book with Jane Amidon.[5]

Kiley's immense body of landscape design awaits a full critical assessment. His late effort with Amidon is a valuable statement of his thoughts and a thorough and well-illustrated documentation of his work. However, as its subtitle, *The Complete Works of America's Master Landscape Architect*, indicates, it is more a catalog and a celebration than a critique. More critical studies are beginning to appear in recent monographs and essays, but much remains to be done.[6]

The present publication is most certainly not "*the* Kiley book"—a reality to be hoped for but as yet unseen. Instead it pairs a reprint of *The Work of Dan Kiley: A Dialogue on Design Theory*—a transcript of a symposium held at the University of Virginia's School of Architecture in 1982—with an assemblage of four critical essays on Kiley's landscape architecture: two of them new, two of them revised versions of essays previously published. Kiley's own symposium presentation constitutes one of the most succinct and lucid accounts of his design philosophy. A lively discussion with panelists Laurie Olin, David Streatfield, Reuben Rainey, and the student audience augmented the plethora of ideas offered by Kiley in his talk. As a rare comprehensive view of thoughts and designs, these proceedings remain a valuable resource; unfortunately, the original publication—which enjoyed only a very limited circulation—is long out of print.

The essays by John Beardsley, Gregg Bleam, Elizabeth K. Meyer, and Marc Treib at times trek across the same terrain—with especially frequent visits to the exquisite and iconic Miller garden in Columbus, Indiana. Such unavoidable overlap is to be welcomed, given the subtlety and sophistication of Kiley's work and its power to invite varying interpretations. Like most Kiley landscapes, the qualities and meanings of the Miller garden can no more be exhausted in a single reading or interpretation than a painting by Pablo Picasso, a symphony by Gustav Mahler, or a play by Eugene O'Neill.

We hope that this revisiting of an animated symposium of twenty-six years ago, accompanied by contemporary commentary, will inform the current generation and stimulate further critical engagement with the legacy of one of America's great landscape architects.

1 Harry Wolf, "On Collaboration with Dan Kiley," in Dan Kiley and Jane Amidon, *Dan Kiley: The Complete Works of America's Master Landscape Architect* (Boston: Bulfinch Press, 1999), p. 17.

2 Garrett Eckbo, Dan U. Kiley, and James C. Rose: "Landscape Design in the Urban Environment," *Architectural Record* (May 1939), reprinted in Marc Treib, ed., *Modern Landscape Architecture: A Critical Review* (Cambridge, Mass.: MIT Press, 1993), pp. 78-82; "Landscape Design in the Rural Environment," *Architectural Record* (August 1939), reprinted in Treib, *Modern Landscape Architecture*, pp. 83–87; "Landscape Design in the Primeval Environment," *Architectural Record* (February 1940), reprinted in Treib, *Modern Landscape Architecture*, pp. 88–91.

3 See Kiley's brief early essay, "Nature: The Source of All Design," in *Landscape Architecture* (January 1963), pp. 8–10.

4 Dan Kiley, in Warren T. Byrd, Jr. and Reuben M. Rainey, eds., *The Work of Dan Kiley: A Dialogue on Design Theory* (Charlottesville: The University of Virginia, School of Architecture, 1983), p. 30. Kiley's essay of 1963 cited in note 3 is an exception to his warning about not theorizing before practice, since it was written rather early in his career.

5 Kiley and Amidon, *Dan Kiley, The Complete Works*.

6 In addition to the essays in this volume by Marc Treib and Gregg Bleam, which originally appeared in *Landscape Journal* and Treib, *Modern Landscape Architecture* respectively, see Gary R. Hilderbrand, *The Miller Garden: Icon of Modernism* (Cambridge, Mass.: Spacemaker Press, 1999); William S. Saunders, ed., *Daniel Urban Kiley, The Early Gardens* (New York: Princeton Architectural Press, 1999); *Landscape Design: Works of Dan Kiley, Process Architecture No. 33* (October 1982); *Dan Kiley: Landscape Design II, in Step with Nature, Process Architecture No. 108* (February 1993); Jory Johnson and Felice Frankel, "The Miller House," in *Modern Landscape Architecture: Redefining the Garden* (New York:, 1991), pp. 112–127; Michael Van Valkenburgh, "Two Views of Landscape Design," *Orion Nature Quarterly* (1984/85), and "Dan Kiley," in *Built Landscapes: Gardens in the Northeast* (Brattleboro, VT: Brattleboro Museum and Art Center, 1984); and Peter Walker and Melanie Simo, "The Lone Classicist," in *Invisible Gardens: The Search for Modernism in the American Landscape* (Cambridge, Mass.: MIT Press, 1994), pp. 170–197.

THE WORK OF DAN KILEY

A Dialogue on Design Theory

**PROCEEDINGS OF
THE FIRST ANNUAL SYMPOSIUM ON LANDSCAPE ARCHITECTURE**

The University of Virginia
School of Architecture
Division of Landscape Architecture

Campbell Hall
February 6, 1982

INTRODUCTORY REMARKS
Jaquelin Robertson

LECTURE
Dan Kiley

PANEL DISCUSSION
Moderator:
Harry Porter
Panelists:
Dan Kiley
Laurie Olin
David Streatfield
Reuben Rainey

/ A /

Foreword

to *The Work of Dan Kiley: A Dialogue on Design Theory*, 1982

Warren T. Byrd, Jr.

Reuben M. Rainey

Editors

This work is an edited account of the first Annual Symposium on Landscape Architecture sponsored by the School of Architecture of the University of Virginia. The symposium was held on February 6, 1982, at the School of Architecture.

The purpose of this symposium and the ones that will follow is to provide an opportunity for leading figures in the field of landscape architecture to interpret their work and discuss the values and influences which inform it. Such discussion should contribute to the contemporary dialogue on design theory within the profession as well as its allied disciplines of architecture, planning, and architectural history. The publication of the symposium proceedings will also serve to record the thought of distinguished contemporary landscape architects and thus provide primary source materials for the history of the profession.

The format of the first Annual Symposium was as follows: Dan Kiley presented his approach to design in the morning session, illustrating his remarks with slides. He touched on such topics as his design education, the influence of historical precedent on his work, the values which inform his designs, and his roots in the New England landscape. Kiley then participated in an afternoon panel discussion which further explored the intentions and implications of his designs.

This account of the symposium includes the introduction of Dan Kiley by Jaquelin Robertson, Dean of the School of Architecture, the University of Virginia, Dan Kiley's morning presentation, and the afternoon panel discussion. Panel members, in addition to Kiley, included: Harry W. Porter, Jr., moderator, Chairman of the Division of Landscape Architecture, the University of Virginia; Laurie Olin, Assistant Professor of Landscape

TITLE PAGE,
*THE WORK OF DAN KILEY:
A DIALOGUE ON DESIGN
THEORY*, 1982.

Architecture, the University of Pennsylvania, and principal Hanna/Olin, Inc.; David Streatfield, Assistant Professor of Landscape Architecture, the University of Washington; and Reuben M. Rainey, Assistant Professor of Landscape Architecture, the University of Virginia. What follows is an edited transcription of the tape-recording of the day's sessions. The editors have removed the redundancies and ambiguities typical of such spontaneous oral discussions and have added illustrations which support Kiley's talk. Also, they have deleted points in the discussion which did not receive ample development or clarification. However, they have sought to preserve the spontaneity and conversational tone of the symposium. One can hardly think of a greater injustice to Dan Kiley than to transform the wit and freshness of his Gaelic discourse into deadly academic prose. This account, we trust, conveys the spirit of that Saturday in February, but more importantly, captures some of the essence of Dan Kiley: his background, his intentions, and his joy in his work.

It is most appropriate that Dan Kiley inaugurate the symposium series. He has quietly been at the forefront of contemporary American landscape architecture since he collaborated with Garrett Eckbo and James Rose on articles written for *Architectural Record* beginning in May 1939. These first attempts at trying to understand modern trends in landscape architecture as they paralleled architecture and the arts were soon realized in several of Kiley's major commissions. The Jefferson National Expansion Memorial in St. Louis with Eero Saarinen (1947-48), the Irwin Miller Residence, Columbus, Indiana, with Eero Saarinen and Kevin Roche (1953), Dulles

Airport with Eero Saarinen (1958), the Oakland Museum with Kevin Roche (1962), and current work with I. M. Pei and others are not only expressions of a complementary modernism but are most significant as essays in collaboration. They are dialogues between landscape architect and architect, the vernacular and the "designed," nature and man, earth and sky, past and present.

Kiley's understanding of architectural language speaks most clearly through his designs. They are characterized by a strong geometry, clear axial organization, bold architectonic massing of plant materials, crisply articulated walls and terraces, and interlocking spaces. It is no wonder he works so often and so well with leading architectural practitioners. They understand that he understands. Here one is reminded of such lasting and forceful collaborations as that of Le Nôtre and Le Vau at Vaux-le-Vicomte and Versailles. This analogy seems all the more appropriate as Dan Kiley holds Le Nôtre as one of his highest sources of inspiration. Both are concerned with the manipulation of space: consequently the result is an architecture of the landscape, the creation of an architecture outdoors.

For Kiley, landscape architecture is an art that recognizes the nature of nature and the nature of man. It is an art that sees man as nature, not merely a part of nature. As Dan Kiley says, "Man is nature." And though man as designer is a source of design inspiration, so too are nature and the vernacular. These additional sources of design guidance are more difficult to "see" in his completed works, but are no less important. The meeting of architectural form with that which nature inherently "designs" (forests, meadows) and that which the non-designer brings to everyday life (farms, villages) is the achievement of Dan Kiley's landscapes. He sees "the walk in nature" as "exciting, original and dynamic" and states that his work has sought "to create a man-made scene having those attributes and characteristics." It is the "idea" and "spirit of nature" that is of concern, not precise replications or creation of mock-natural scenes. His art recalls the image of hedgerows and country roads, the meeting of the geometry of orchards with the natural roll of the land; it translates the sensation of passing through the deep shade of a sugar maple grove and bursting out upon a meadow. Consequently his design vocabulary is concerned less with individual plants and isolated things and more with the gathered momentum of fields and forests, a sustained line or lines in the landscape. His palette is variously composed of groves, bosques, allées, rows, arbors, pergolas, and trelliage.

If one dates his practice of landscape architecture from the days of his apprenticeship with Warren Manning, Kiley has been at his art for fifty years. His command of form and material at a variety of scales and his previously-mentioned capacity to collaborate with the distinguished architects of his day have kept him in the forefront of the profession. His consummate ability to integrate architecture with the natural and urban environment, which is grounded in a subtle understanding of the unity of human beings with nature, remains the hallmark of his work. It is a work which is constantly renewing itself in each new situation, yet is informed by the accomplishments of the past. It stands as one of the most brilliant achievements of contemporary landscape architecture. Our thanks to all those students and faculty who had

a part in making the symposium a successful venture. Particular thanks are due Jane Jacobs and members of the graduate landscape architecture classes of 1982 and 1983 for help in organizational and logistical matters; to Roxanne Brouse and Lisa Pennypacker for their contributions both during the symposium, running projectors and tape recorders, and afterwards, transcribing the proceedings; to Sue Rainey for help with the editing; and to Thelma Thurston for the typing.

We must also recognize those "players" without whom we simply would have had no symposium: to Jaquelin Robertson for his warm introduction and, in particular, for being so supportive of the entire endeavor from inception to conclusion; to Harry Porter, who expertly conducted the afternoon's discussion; and to the panel: Laurie Olin and David Streatfield, for their dogged pursuit of the reasons why. Finally, we are indebted most of all to Dan Kiley for his presence in our symposium that Saturday in February 1982. His presence, like his work, has deeply influenced us all.

/ B /

Introduction

Jaquelin Robertson

Good morning. This is our first landscape symposium, and I think it is going to be a very interesting one. I want to say a few things about Dan Kiley which have to do both with his "formal" curriculum vitae and his "informal" one.

When I was in Tehran some years ago, my secretary came in one day and said, "Mr. Robertson, there's a very special kind of man outside waiting to see you." I asked, "Who is he?" and she replied, "I couldn't get his name, but he says he knows you and that he's a landscape architect." "What does he look like?" She thought for a moment, said, "Well, he looks like a troubadour who just came in from the Austrian Tyrol. He's very healthy looking and very spry and has a sparkle in his eye." I knew then–"It's Dan Kiley."

Dan Kiley has been a hero of mine ever since I went into architecture. In the late 1950s and early 1960s he seemed to be the only practicing landscape architect, in this country at least, who understood that landscape was not only the cheapest, but also the most beautiful "architecture" and that, in fact, cities and places were best made with this kind of "green architecture." He seemed to me a landscape master builder, and he looked much, much better to me than about 99 percent of our best architects, as an architect making a real architecture with trees and paving and planting and water.

When I was a student at Yale, Kiley was known but mysterious, one of those we all wanted to find out more about; we hoped for him in New Haven as a design critic. We never got him, unfortunately.

Later when I went to New York to work for Ed Barnes, Ed and Dan were doing several projects together and it was extraordinarily exciting for me at that time to finally

/ B-1 /
DAN KILEY, NCNB BANK PLAZA, TAMPA, FLORIDA, 1988.
/ AARON KILEY, OFFICE OF DAN KILEY /

get close to this eccentric man, who, as my Iranian secretary had noticed, looked like a cross between a lep-
rechaun and a Tyrolean ski instructor. Dan is quite a
different sort of person. It's always like a vacation for
me to be with him, always light; nearly always unexpected; and most importantly, fun; therefore education-
al in a most profound way.

Dan was born in Boston. He went, unfortunately, to
Harvard; served, unfortunately, in the U.S. Army Corps
of Engineers (it's still hard for me to believe that), and
then did something that I find very interesting: he earned
the Legion of Merit for the design and construction of
the Nuremberg courtroom trials.

He has, in the course of a busy professional life, served
on an extraordinary number of advisory boards, such
as the one on Pennsylvania Avenue, for which he did a
major piece of design. He has also been a member of
the Cambridge Redevelopment Authority and the State
of Vermont Design Board. He has worked all over the
United States and many places abroad—from Snowbird
to Iran—and was for a time the Landscape Architect in
Residence at the American Academy in Rome.

From the beginning, Dan has been fortunate to have
worked on what could only be called "blue-chip" projects
with the very best people. It hasn't been by luck, because
he is the best. He and Eero Saarinen won the Jefferson
Memorial competition in St. Louis in 1947–48. He then
began as a kind of in-house consultant to Irwin Miller
of Cummins Engines in Columbus, Indiana. He is
responsible for the landscaping at the U.S. Air Force

Academy and at Dulles Airport, in some ways the most lyrical piece of large-scale landscaping that I know of in this country. (I think the landscaping wins over the building at Dulles, it just seems to make the building work. That is, the building without it would not be what it is.) He did the beautiful Third Block on Independence Mall in Philadelphia, the John F. Kennedy Library in Boston, and that very nice court at Lincoln Center, the long court around the pool with the Henry Moore sculpture, as well as the beautiful hidden garden at the Rockefeller Institute on York Avenue in New York City. If you read down a list of big, prominent projects in the United States by first-class architects, very often Dan has collaborated on them. In my own view, it is the landscape architecture which is the thread that ties all of those projects together. Essentially, Dan Kiley, as I said at the beginning, made urban architecture with trees a reality again in this country and because of this became very important for a generation of young architects and landscape architects who were looking for that kind of expression, that attitude (Laurie Olin, one of the very best "younger" landscape architect/architects, was one of those).

Dan is an architect, then, a landscape architect, a planner, an urban designer, an inveterate tinkerer, a gardener. And, in that sense, he's very much like the founder of the University of Virginia, Thomas Jefferson, who I think would be chuckling and rather jolly to have Dan here this morning. Dan, as Dean of the School of Architecture, and in Mr. Jefferson's absence, I would like to welcome you, the dean of Landscape Architecture in the United States.

/ **B-2** / *opposite*
DAN KILEY, AT THE BEACH, CAPE COD, 1938.
/ ENVIRONMENTAL DESIGN ARCHIVES, UNIVERSITY OF CALIFORNIA, BERKELEY /
/ **B-3** / *right*
DAN KILEY AT HIS HOME AND OFFICE IN CHARLOTTE, VERMONT, 1999.
/ MARC TREIB /

/ C /

Lecture

Dan Kiley

I like to travel lightly, step lightly on this earth [figure C-1]. I like, as Henry David Thoreau said, to live in a tent, as it were, in this world, hitting only the high points. I leave the low, katabatic valleys to the regional planners and ecologists, since they insist on staying in those dammed-up areas, and I propose that the one good thing Olmsted said was "aptness"–things should be apt, appropriate. On two occasions I was on television with mayors in Canada. One was in Calgary, and, as they usually do, the mayor turned to me and said, "How do you like our fair city?" I said, "It's quite a nice city, but don't you know it's in the wrong place? No Indian would even camp on the floodplains of the Bow River because of this katabatic zone of unhealth." And then the mayor of Edmonton, where we were going to do a project in the center of town, asked, "How did you like our fair city?" I said, "It's okay, but I understand you're going to tear down the only good buildings here–the post office and the courthouse." So, my developer client was getting a little worried that I might lose him the Calgary job. We finally ended up designing, as architects, the four highest buildings in Calgary, the lower levels of which have to be in this katabatic valley.

Just a little more on this business of cities in the wrong place: Almost every single city in this country that has levees around it, costing billions of dollars, the pride of the Corps of Engineers, is breached almost every year. All those cities are located where the Indians told the people not to build. We did a river study in Dayton, Ohio, where they have miles of levees, but wait until the spring. You'll see the Mississippi flooded again, the Ohio flooded. It's just what Olmsted was talking about, aptness–those things are in the wrong place.

I think that it's very important for young people, for everybody really, to prepare for design. I've always felt that I cannot separate my life and my work, and the more we get it together in this fractured world environment, the better. Emerson wrote a beautiful essay called "The Whole Man," which inspired me very much right from the beginning. Indeed, the basis for starting your career can be many different points of departure, and religion and philosophy are very good ones. One of the ideas of which I shall speak is you as part of the universe.

For a short time I worked in Washington, D.C., in the U.S. Housing Authority and did some work with Lou Kahn, but I quickly moved up to northern New England, first to New Hampshire. I remember Eero Saarinen saying to me, "Dan, you should locate in Chicago and control the country." I said, "Eero, I'd rather control it from New Hampshire"—which I didn't, of course.

Reuben Rainey came to talk to me when he was teaching religion at Middlebury College. He had decided to study landscape architecture and asked me, "Which school should I go to?" I said, "Well, really, it depends upon the person completely, because there's no school that is clearly best. But you should go where you think you'd love to be." I think that's the big thing. If you love what you're doing, if you love where you are, and if you love the whole scene, it's bound to come together. And nature's with you all the time.

Fortunately, I had very little education. I was very lucky. Number one, I was too poor. I had to work. Number two, I was too dumb. In high school, I only took the thin books home (they were easy to carry), and walked my girlfriend through the Arnold Arboretum, where I learned all about the trees, and also the birds. It was in the middle of the Depression; there was no work anywhere. I wanted very much to get a job in interior design, in an interior decorator's shop, because I loved furniture. I love the design of furniture. Instead a friend of mine got a job there, but was completely uninterested.

In desperation, I finally wrote to all the landscape architects in Boston, including John Nolan, a Boston city planner, Howard Hill Blossom—there's a good name for a landscape architect—and finally Warren H. Manning. I still have Manning's letter, written in hen scratchings, in which he said, "My dear young man," and offered me a job without pay. I felt very lucky. He was a lovely, wonderful man. He was not a great designer; rather he was a philosopher of the land and one who helped establish many of the early parks. One story he always told concerned Harrisburg, Pennsylvania, where he was trying to assemble land for a park in the center of the town on the river. The mayor, Vance McCormick, said, "Manning, Pennsylvania Dutch just don't give land." Manning, who had a white beard and looked like Santa Claus, tried to get people to give land. Not only did they give, but Vance McCormick was the one who gave the first and the most. They got that open park.

As a kid I would drive Manning all over the place in a Model A convertible. I really learned many things from him, particularly about plant materials, because he was a great expert. He gave me advice on two points. Incidentally, he was one of the founders of the American Society of Landscape Architects and was president twice. The two things he said were, "Don't join the American Society of Landscape Architects," which I didn't, of course. (I did join the A.I.A. for the insurance, and then I quit.) And "Don't go to Harvard." I disobeyed that one. I did go to Harvard as a special student in 1936, and stayed long enough to know I didn't want to go anymore. That took two years. So I never got a degree. And I've had no regrets. My best course at Harvard was Music I, which was not part of the design curriculum.

I think what we're talking about is the poetry of space–that's what landscape design is about. We need to develop sensitivity, which is another reason I like to live in the north country and practice what I preach: live on the land–become sensitive to land and not stumble over the rocks or step on the hepaticas. I have had great ecologists, planners, and intellectuals walk up the hill with me. They're walking up and their minds are still back in cities thinking of other things; meanwhile the whole land disappears, as do any ideas of nature and space.

Also recalling David Streatfield's lecture yesterday on pioneer landscapes in the Pacific Northwest, it occurs to me that one of our problems is boundaries. When we came and grabbed all that land from the Indians, they didn't think of land as being owned by anybody, with a line around it. Thoreau said something once: I can't quote it exactly, but the idea was that there was a surveyor, surveying the land, knocking in stakes and getting his angles, and meanwhile the Angel of Death was fluttering in back of him. He was like a miser, cutting and dividing part of the universe, thinking it his.

We are one with the universe. Man is nature. Is that not exciting to realize? It's not man *and* nature. It's not man *with* nature. Man *is* nature, just like the trees. Both live and grow. I see man in his highest civilized, and hopefully cultured, way being evident in his imprint on the universe. This is the fulfilling idea of the universe and the world: that man is elevated and projected into his highest possibility, using his talents both as an organizer and as a poet of design.

I think of design in the landscape as being like a walk in nature. It's all there, really, instead of copying the end result of a natural process, which the landscape architecture profession has done, especially ever since the mid or even early eighteenth century. From then on, landscape architects were always copying something. But the walk in nature is exciting and original, a fresh experience where you are going through a deep wood, maybe a grove of beech trees, then you come into an open meadow and you walk up the hill and then you come into the sugar maples, or "sugarbush," as they call it in Vermont, and you walk through that. You squeeze in between the trunks, and it's always moving and changing spatially. It's dynamic. This is the thing that intrigued and excited me right from the beginning. What I've been trying to do in my work is create a man-made scene having those attributes or characteristics.

I have been criticized a lot because my work is geometric. I say, "Well, what do you want me to do, go back to the kind of work I did when I was eighteen?" Because that's what they are referring to–little copies of nature. It's not that everything comes out geometric; it depends on site conditions, program, and other concerns. Actually even though much of our work is not geometric, most of the work I show probably is. However, because it's geometric in plan doesn't mean that the space is static; hopefully the space continues to flow.

I'll begin by showing you pictures of how I live because I think it's nice to see all of that, and it's important in understanding why I do a certain kind of work. I do live in the midst of nature. Some people who copy nature and criticize me for not doing so, don't know how I live. This is where Anne and I and our eight children first lived in Vermont, on Lake Champlain. Our house is on Wing's Point. We bought it from Sir Wilfred Grenfell, the missionary to Labrador and explorer. My second eldest son is named Pusstoe after Sir Wilfred Grenfell's cat. Our house overlooks the lake and beautiful limestone cliffs and arborvitae forest. This is the starting line of white cedar, or arborvitae, which continues north. This is down on the lake edge. When our office was only four people, we worked in this little boathouse. When it got hot, we'd slip out the French doors onto the rocks and then swim away and cool off.

When we first moved here with our eight children, Anne and I swam out from the shore to this island. It doesn't look that far, but it's a half mile. We both swam, leaving the eight children together all naked on the shore. Then we swam back. I beat her by one arm stroke. She's quite an athlete.

I sail these rugged waters in my English sloop designed by Lawrence Giles and built in Christchurch, England. I believe in getting the things I love. That boat is one. And then this car, the Morgan, is my love. Everything you love really works out for you. If I ever have to sell these kinds of things, I'd get ten times what they cost originally.

We moved to East Charlotte, Vermont, eight miles from where we started at the lake. This place is just at the foothills of the Green Mountains. The mountains extend across most of the state of Vermont. And Mount Mansfield, where we ski, is up here. The farm in East Charlotte was an 1810 square house that I added on to. [figure C-2]. In 1963, we planted two rows of Lombardy poplars, one row of sugar maples, and pairs of quaking aspens. Most of these trees, except for the sugar maples, are trees landscape architects don't plant because they don't live long enough.

This is the farm, which is now our office. You see, there's no sign of work there at all. I don't mind looking at work, but I hate to do too much of it. If you ease your mind, everything happens right.

Then after all the children had grown up—they didn't move away from Vermont, except two—we decided that the house was too big for us. It's 120 feet long and varies from 36 feet wide. So I built a new house. I should have had Jack Robertson do it, but I didn't know him so well then. I designed it, as they say, on an envelope, and gradually built it. The driveway arrives at this little courtyard of barns, and there's a little pavilion on the way to the house. This is about the biggest white birch I've ever seen.

Since I built the house on the side of the hill instead of on top, I had to build it vertically, to get up high again. The house is oriented to the southeast, completely protected from the west winds. On this side the morning sun comes in benignly and warms the place up.

This is the start of the walk which goes into our house; in the summer it's all thick with plants around the house and cool in there. Out in the court it can be 85 degrees and in the house it will be 70. From the house you can see the Green Mountain line. There's a great big 200-year-old sugar maple here.

The person who inspired me the most is Le Nôtre. I finally had the wonderful opportunity of joining with some of his work on a project in Paris. He did a network —all the chateaus in Paris came together as one regional continuation. We got a project that was an extension of the Champs Elysées. The project itself was pretty awful, but we had the chance to do things with it.

/ C-2 / left
KILEY OFFICE,
CHARLOTTE, VERMONT.
/ GARRETT ECKBO, 1968 /
/ C-3 / opposite left
ANDRÉ LE NÔTRE,
CHÂTEAU DE SCEAUX,
FRANCE, LATE 17th
CENTURY.
/ MARC TREIB /
/ C-4 / opposite right
CHÂTEAU DE VILLANDRY,
FRANCE, 1536, RECREATED
EARLY 20th CENTURY.
/ MARC TREIB /

Here are some thoughts on several of my other projects and some of the things that inspired my work. There was one job in Washington, D.C.–the Gallaudet School for the Deaf. Hugh Jacobsen, the architect in Washington, got them to ask me if I'd be interested in doing it. But he told me, "Go easy on the geometry because you're thought of as a neo-classicist." I said, "Forget the neo." When I gave my presentation, I started off by showing Frederick Law Olmsted, Sr. I didn't show Le Nôtre at all. Sneaky. And I got the job. Thanks to Mr. Olmsted. Incidentally, presentations are very important in work. You can be a little genius in the corner, but no one will ever hear of you. You also have to excite people to do work and keep them going, to get more work.

I took a trip to Europe in 1945, right after World War II. Incidentally, I met Le Corbusier on that trip, in his apartment. Using examples from that trip, I used to give talks to students years ago in which I referred to man's module of 30 feet on center, as in these olive groves near Cordoba in Spain. Because of the folding and intricacies of the land, these turn into ever-changing, varied, and fantastic groves that are very beautiful, I think. The point is that you don't need a lot of ideas, you just need a 30-foot module to start with. Who has designed the perfect square building, for instance? One should start on a simple basis. Get the right diagram.

At the Château de Sceaux, Le Nôtre did this beautiful planting [figure C-3]. Although symmetrical, it has wonderful spatial sequences. The way the poplars move, you see. People say, "Don't plant poplars because they last only 10, 15, or 20 years. But, my God, during that 15 or 20 years, it's heaven. Mine are phasing out now, just as I am, so it works out beautifully.

There again, just the spaces of these strong trees are what landscape design is all about. This is a road right next to Château de Sceaux. I find this powerful. I love it. Trunks can be as close as you want.

The Château de Villandry is composed of miraculous pattern and textures–it's almost Japanese in this area [figure C-4]. And the way the paving is used, and the way the forms work. You know, this could be the most modern scene–and Le Nôtre did it in the seventeenth century. The garden also has this very thin grape arbor, not thick, so the thinness is nice. And the way the littleleaf linden march down and through, probably about 8 to 10 feet on center: it's architecture. Architecture in the land.

When people want to copy these dumb nature scenes, I say, "If you're going to copy, copy your ancestors –the colonial gardens." For instance, the George Wythe House in Williamsburg, where Thomas Jefferson lived when he was studying law with Wythe, who was his mentor. All of the outbuildings and dependencies are organized on a platform of brick with the grass cut neatly. Even the privies are on axis in the formal gardens, with one on either side. And there is also a little arbor made of clipped beech. Another of my favorites is the lovely garden of Mrs. Paul Mellon, one that she designed herself and which includes a pleached allée of crabapple trees.

To discuss some of our work–we begin with the Oakland Museum in Oakland, California [figure C-5]. Incidentally, this was the first job Kevin Roche got after Eero Saarinen died. They interviewed Lou Kahn, Philip Johnson–all the top people. It was crucial for Saarinen's

office to get something like this to keep going. So Kevin made a beautiful presentation showing how the city had developed and how his plan related to the city plan. He decided there should not be a building in this block since the auditorium and the city hall were nearby. So he made the museum all underground in three levels [figures C-5, C-6]. Even the grass panels tilt in. So you can come in at the top, go down under the restaurant, and go down below and out. Then you can walk inside through arbors and up onto the roof. So, our problem was to get the planting that would work within this context. The depth of the soil varied from about eight inches to three feet inside. But there were areas on the perimeter where you could go down to natural grade. Every place we could we put panels of eucalyptus. But we couldn't put high trees everywhere we wanted to because of such shallow soil. So, for example, in a three-foot-deep area we used plants such as Japanese pear.

Existing on the site were a few beautiful, big cedars of Lebanon. Incidentally, I take credit for everything that's there, if it's good. These trees are wonderful. I usually don't tell people I didn't put those trees in there. This is one of the first jobs where we used special soil mix. It's called UC (University of California) Mix #6. All of the watering and feeding is done automatically. When the plants need a shot of something, there are sensors in the soil that let the pump know and it pumps out that material.

Kevin Roche wanted it overgrown, and because of that I planted things very closely. I originally specified on the plan bougainvillea at two feet on center. The park commissioner who was going to have to maintain it said, "You're from the East. That's too close." I knew

he was going to say that beforehand, and I said, "Okay, I'll make them four feet on center." So they turned out four feet on center. They really should be ten feet on center. It's the same way with budgets. I wanted a million to do this job, and we ended up with $500,000. We always get our figures cut in half on every project, so we always double them to start.

The next project is the Irwin Miller house in Columbus, Indiana [figures C-7, C-8]. Eero Saarinen asked me to do this in the early days; Kevin Roche was working with him, and Alexander Girard did the interior. The house was designed in functional blocks, such as the kitchen, the dining room, the master bedroom, and the living room. So I took this same geometry and made rooms outside using trees in groves and allées. And the whole thing becomes a geometry. Mr. Miller didn't want to feel that he was keeping the community out, and yet he wanted privacy, so I said, "Okay, Irwin, we'll put in a hedge with openings, so the space kind of goes in and out, but you can't see in and you don't feel the line going out." Incidentally, there were no plants at all here when we started.

Below to the west we designed a very romantic kind of park in contrast to the geometry near the house. There was supposed to be a Henry Moore here and Rodin's *The Kiss* was to be in a little pavilion. Doug Sampson, who worked for me then, drew *The Kiss* so real that it embarrassed us all a little, so it was never built.

The entrance drive is planted with horse chestnuts and arborvitae hedges as wings. Along the street we planted red maples very close together outside the hedges.

Then, finally, they got a Henry Moore piece, which was placed at the end of the west allée of honey-

/ **C-5** / *opposite left*
DAN KILEY, OAKLAND MUSEUM,
OAKLAND, CALIFORNIA, 1969.
/ MARC TREIB /
/ **C-6** / *opposite right*
OAKLAND MUSEUM,
OAKLAND, CALIFORNIA.
/ MARC TREIB /
/ **C-7** / *above*
DAN KILEY, MILLER GARDEN,
COLUMBUS, INDIANA, 1955.
/ MARC TREIB /
/ **C-8** / *below*
MILLER GARDEN, COLUMBUS,
INDIANA, 1955.
/ ANNE BARNUM /

locusts [see figure C-7]. The house is surrounded by a ten-foot terrace extending out from the house with the same paving on all sides. This podium goes all around, so you have a 25-foot podium from each facade out. It's like an island; the kind of house you don't extend out from, but instead is more like a temple in the round.

Getting the right plant material is many times a matter of luck. In Greenwich, Connecticut, we found an estate where a road was going through, and we were able to buy these saucer magnolias very cheaply. We got six of them and moved them out to Columbus, Indiana.

A swimming pool was added later, around 1963. Additional plantings include two weeping beech, which are like great drapes between the house and the allée. It's good in the summer, because the hot Indiana sun beats down. We also planted a redbud grove with crushed rock underneath.

Close to the Miller house, we had the opportunity to do another house for a man named Clarence Hamilton. When I first went to him, I said, "Clarence, you should sell your house (it was just an ordinary suburban house looking onto the road), and I'll get you the best architect in the world and a new site." He said, "Well, Muriel likes it here so well, and we really want to go to town on the landscape." The last I heard, the landscape costs were probably over $150,000. This was twenty years ago [figures C-9, C-10].

The garden includes a bosque of littleleaf lindens with groundcover and is enclosed by walls seven feet high. Along the wall are what I call the "Spanish Fountains." There's a little pavilion here and down here another screened pavilion; then there's a dining place, including a

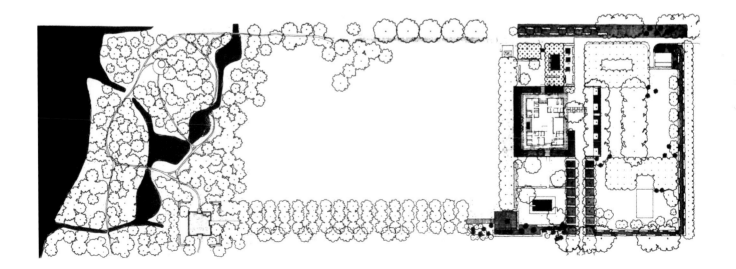

fireplace with a lily pond behind it. You can sit in there and look up this little allée and out at the swimming pool.

I think that structures—pergolas and arbors—are wonderful in the landscape because they encompass three dimensions and give shade and shadow, and yet they don't cost very much.

La Défense is the plaza project in Paris I mentioned earlier [figure C-11]. When we went there the paving load in this large area (incidentally, it's a kilometer long) was planned to be only 110 pounds per square foot. We told them that they needed trees, and in order to get the trees we got them to eliminate a whole level of parking so we could have six or eight feet of soil in there. They finally did it after great persuasion.

From the plaza restaurant you see these large fountains and the waterfall. You drive in below and see the waterfall and all the colors in the refracted light. And then the fountains go way up, and you have an orchestra of water effects. The pool tile and fountains were designed by the sculptor Agam.

The next project is the Ford Foundation in New York City [figures C-12, C-13]. My original idea here was to have a grove of eucalyptus that would grow 130 feet high and McGeorge Bundy could peek out through the leaves. But knowing that these would never grow and amount to much, I decided I had better get some big southern magnolias, which we moved from Richmond, Virginia, and put into place without conditioning them. They weren't doing that sort of thing then. This planting survived and is going on 15 years now. The first year we had a change of flowers every two weeks. It was quite exciting every two weeks to see some new color scheme. But that got a little heavy on maintenance.

A more current job that we've been working with Ed Barnes on is the Dallas Art Museum. The entrance drive passes four big live oaks, and we have live oak groves all around and walls with waterfalls and sculptures on them. There are interior groves besides.

The latest project, which we have just finished, is a new plaza at the Detroit Art Institute. It includes fountains and a water staircase that you walk up around and behind. It was very dramatic at the opening. We were sitting up there, and the mayor spoke. Henry Ford and his wife were there, and there was no water on. Then this group of young dancers, like *West Side Story*, came out. They were dressed in various colors and started dancing all over the steps. Then at the end the water came on and they started dancing in the water. It was really quite something.

At Dulles Airport, everything is on a module, mostly for maintenance [figure C-14]. The planting is all material derived from hedgerows in Virginia and put into a man-made scene, making a spatial arrangement with the terminal. The planting consists of blocks of big trees, such as oaks, which are going to be 80 feet high (they're about 35 to 40 feet now), and red cedars that are planted on a regular module and mowed in between. There are also quaking aspen in the median strip. You make the module, but then you take out plants every so often, and it turns out to be a loose pattern that has a maintenance line.

We worked with Paul Cannon of CRS on a project in Columbus, Indiana, called Indiana Bell [figure C-15]. It's a structure they have filled with wires and equipment; very few people have to be in there. The design is an aluminum armature, a vertical space frame, with five

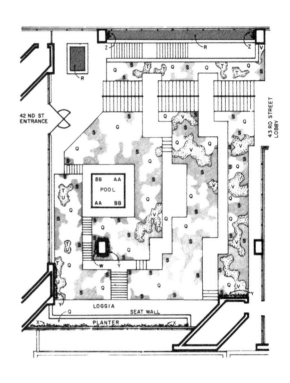

/ **C-9** / *opposite left*
**DAN KILEY, HAMILTON
GARDEN, COLUMBUS,
INDIANA, 1965.**
THE CENTRAL ALLEE
AND PAVILION.
/ MARC TREIB /

/ **C-10** / *opposite right*
HAMILTON GARDEN.
THE PERIMETER PERGOLA
WITH DIAGONAL ELEMENTS.
/ MARC TREIB /

/ **C-11** / *above*
**DAN KILEY, DALLE DE LA
DEFENSE, PARIS, FRANCE,
1978. CENTRAL PROMENADE.**
/ MARC TREIB /

/ **C-12** / *above right*
**DAN KILEY,
LANDSCAPE ARCHITECT;
ROCHE DINKELOO,
ARCHITECTS;
FORD FOUNDATION BUILDING,
NEW YORK CITY, 1964, PLAN.**
/ OFFICE OF DAN KILEY /

/ **C-13** / *below right*
**FORD FOUNDATION
BUILDING, NEW YORK CITY,
CENTRAL ATRIUM.**
/ GARRETT ECKBO /

different vines climbing through it. When you're walking along the sidewalk, you also get the reflections of the plants on the building, and you get a soft effect rather than just reflected glass coming at you. The vines are doing very well; they're almost up at the top now. We put five different kinds of vines, all shooting to heaven. The base is planted to ground cover and a double row of street trees.

In another project in Columbus, Indiana, the Irwin Union Bank and Trust Company, you drive through a grove of trees to deposit or withdraw money rather than sitting in the hot sun [figure C-16].

The Third Block of Independence Mall in Philadelphia I call an architectural forest [figures C-17, C-18]. We planted 700 honey-locusts. The design was derived from work by Thomas Holme, who was William Penn's surveyor. He laid out the city of Philadelphia with a center square and four additional squares. We took that design thought and repeated it three times. We proposed satellite fountains in all these places, too, which they never would let me build because they thought they'd get filled with trash. The reason they allowed all 700 trees was because a man on the board was the forester of the state of Pennsylvania.

That's the end of my talk. Thank you very much for listening and being so patient. I know it's Saturday morning, and I've drenched you with geometry.

/ **C-14** / *opposite left*
DAN KILEY, DULLES AIRPORT,
HERNDON, VIRGINIA, 1963.
/ DAN KILEY /
/ **C-15** / *opposite right above*
DAN KILEY, INDIANA BELL,
COLUMBUS, INDIANA, 1974.
/ MARC TREIB /
/ **C-16** / *opposite right below*
DAN KILEY, IRWIN UNION
BANK AND TRUST,
COLUMBUS, INDIANA, 1955.
/ MARC TREIB /

/ **C-17** /
DAN KILEY, THIRD BLOCK,
INDEPENDENCE MALL,
PHILADELPHIA,
PENNSYLVANIA, 1963.
CROSS SECTION.
/ FRANCES LOEB LIBRARY,
HARVARD GRADUATE
SCHOOL OF DESIGN,
HEREAFTER FLL, HGSD /
/ **C-18** /
THIRD BLOCK, INDEPENDENCE
MALL.
/ OFFICE OF DAN KILEY /

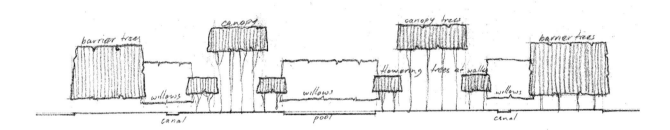

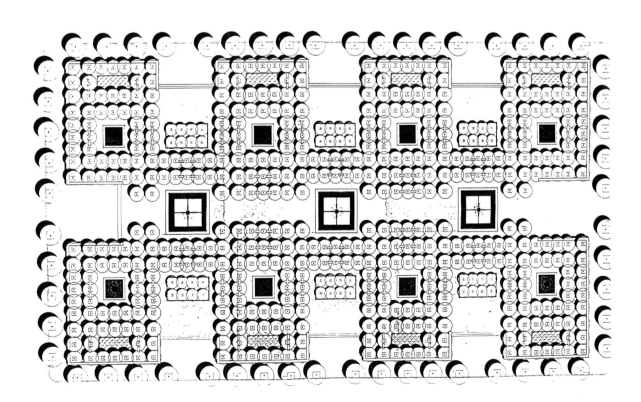

/ D /
Panel Discussion

Harry Porter, Moderator
Dan Kiley
Laurie Olin
Reuben M. Rainey
David Streatfield

HARRY PORTER: The purpose of this question and answer period is actually to draw out more from Dan Kiley. That's why Reuben Rainey, David Streatfield, and Laurie Olin were invited here to be on this panel. Reuben Rainey is a graduate of Columbia University and received his doctoral degree in Philosophy of Religion. After teaching at Columbia University and Middlebury College, he studied landscape architecture at the University of Virginia. He began teaching here about three years ago. Laurie Olin is a graduate of the University of Washington, where he received his degree in architecture. He is presently a member of the firm Hanna/Olin in Philadelphia and New York, and is also a member of the landscape architecture faculty of the Graduate School of Fine Arts at the University of Pennsylvania. He is an artist, an architect, a landscape architect, and, I think, one of the finest practitioners and teachers in the country.

David Streatfield earned his degree in architecture from Brighton College of Art in England, and his master's in landscape architecture from the University of Pennsylvania. He practiced in Philadelphia with the landscape architecture firm of Collins and Dutoe and has taught at Clemson, Michigan State, and the University of California at Berkeley. He is now in charge of the graduate program of landscape architecture at the University of Washington. He is highly regarded in the academic community, especially for his writings and teachings in history and theory, and obviously we value his judgment and his insight enough to invite him from across the continent to be here for this particular session. The procedure for this discussion, then, will be to have the panel ask Dan Kiley questions, and after they have had their opportunity, I'd like to give the audience a chance to ask questions.

/ D-1 /
DAN KILEY,
KIMMEL GARDEN,
SALISBURY, CONNECTICUT,
1996.
/ MARC TREIB /

REUBEN RAINEY: Dan, I want to pick up on some remarks you made this morning about your background. You spoke of your years at Harvard: that you were there for two years and liked Music I the best, that you felt it was the only course that was worthwhile. But you didn't mention that while you were there you helped make some very important history of landscape architecture, in your collaborative writings with Garrett Eckbo and Jim Rose. This is an event which has not been studied very much; there's not much information on it. So I wish you would reminisce about your days at Harvard and speak of what you didn't like about the curriculum, what you rejected, and also about the positive things—the influences that led the three of you to develop the ideas that you explored at that time.

DAN KILEY: I left Harvard in 1938 and was wed in 1942; I was in Washington just at the start of World War II, and Anne and I were at a party, and this girl came up in stocking feet–she was on tiptoe–and said, "Oh, you are a very famous architect–you started *Task* magazine"–which I didn't, but *Task* magazine was kind of a radical magazine that not only architecture and landscape students but other people in Harvard were putting their ideas and thinking into. When I went to Harvard, I was very naive. All I had done was work for Warren Manning. So the important thing of going there was that I found out somewhat what the field was all about, and I also met Jim Rose and Garrett Eckbo. I think meeting them was more important than anything I learned or studied there. I did learn to draw somewhat, though not too well. I said to Walt Chambers, who taught the construction course I took and sat in front of the class reading from a book about different kinds of mixes and road material, "Just give me the book. Let me read it. I don't enjoy sitting here and having you read me the book, because I can read too." It was still a good construction course, although the funny thing is you never use any of that–especially like vertical and horizontal curves. I remember one problem: you know, where you have an interchange on an interstate highway, and you have to get something under the bridge. I never could quite get the contours to work out–the truck always got stuck under there.

I had a disadvantage in that I hadn't been to undergraduate school, and most of the people there had already gotten their bachelor's degrees in landscape architecture. They had pre-training in all of those techniques and approaches, and I was at a great disadvantage. I must say I didn't do very well. As a matter of fact, the best mark I got, I guess, was in Music I after all. But it was stimulating, and Garrett, Jim, and I were kind of the outcasts in relation to the faculty. I think that you have to take chances, and go out and do what you feel. You can't be "safe," like doing things for the faculty and all that. I'd had it after two years and left. That's the best move I made.

I'm trying to think of something good that happened… One thing that set everybody back was that the history of landscape architecture course was so dull and so bad that we just hated anything to do with the past. In some

RAINEY: Could I just pursue a point—why were you considered radical? What was it that set you off against the faculty?

STREATFIELD: Dan, something in what you've just said really intrigues me, because I went to school in the early fifties in England in what I considered at that time to be an incredibly old-fashioned, antiquated architecture school—Brighton College of Art. It's the last vestige of the Beaux-Arts system in architecture. And I hated it as a student. Yet, as I look back on it now, I realize that there was a great deal of strength in that teaching, because it exposed us to a whole discipline, a whole vocabulary, and a language of designing which we had to learn. I think most of us rejected it ideologically, as you did, at the time. Yet I think that of all the landscape architects who have practiced in this country since the 1940s a real sense of the past is most clearly evident in your work—I see you as being a very different designer from, say, Garrett Eckbo and James Rose. From their later writings one has the distinct impression that what they were trying to do was toss out everything that had the remotest connection with the past. Yet in your work, one has what I would describe as a deliciously exciting poetic sense of the spirit of the past living again in the present and refreshing it, sort of surging through it.

STREATFIELD: You said it yourself this morning; you talked about the continuity of the past. And that's really what I'm getting at—because surely the Beaux-Arts system was a link with the past. It was trying to expose students to what now I think we think of still as a living language, something which hasn't died. And yet you said just a moment ago that it had died. What I don't understand is why you didn't respond to that living language when you were a student.

ways that happened to be good, when Gropius had just come in, cutting off the past right like that. But it took me ten years to finally realize that something that was done before was good and interesting, which is, you know, the point; the whole of history coming through and moving by you, and continuing. It's so important, and here the lifeblood of the whole movement was cut off both by boring lectures and by an ideology that nipped the past.

KILEY: The whole regime while I was there and before that was the Beaux-Arts system, where it was all the Academy developing a way to do things, by way of copying the Renaissance. And we were interested in new ways, having discovered and read about Christopher Tunnard in England, the French modern architects in the 1920s in France, and Lewis Mumford. And we kept seeing that there was more to it than the Beaux-Arts approach; that it was too restrictive—where everything was a formula. And so we were trying to experiment and see what's out there, really. It was a little brash and naive, while at the same time it was being so-called radical. It wasn't that bad at all.

KILEY: Can you write that down?

KILEY: I think that's a very good question—excellent. I think the Beaux-Arts system of training is still a superb base to get—you know, the discipline and the knowledge, and the drawing, and all that. The two best people who worked for me in my office were Europeans who had that as a base of training—they're both architects, too.

And none of the Americans who came to get a job with me or worked with me could equal that kind of base training. I think the problem with it was that it was a dead end—it was only in and of itself, and so it ended there. It didn't free, and say, "Now you move from your base." And I think that was the very important part of fracturing it, cutting it out, and looking freshly at a whole new freedom of space. The Beaux-Arts was a two-dimensional design system, and what our departure did was to get up-to-date—get closer to Einstein and what was happening: one, two, three, infinity, rather than one, two, three, stop. And so I think the problem wasn't the training, which was great, but the need of freeing and getting out there and seeing what is now, the point of departure today, with Carl Jung and his contribution to understanding the mind and the collective unconscious and all other developments, scientific and otherwise. You must express something different today than you did 10 years ago, 20 years ago, 100 years ago.

This is a good time to mention the Post-Modernists. There are many very talented, brilliant people who are doing a thing that Charles Jencks calls "Post-Modern." My concern is that the Post-Modern should be an organic development, a continuity from the past. It shouldn't be a misplaced wing—instead of having a wing on each side, there shouldn't be two wings on one side. That's like one hand clapping. And so I always say it's lucky that Philip Johnson isn't designing airplanes. I mean, the cocktail lounge would be fine, but the plane wouldn't keep going. I know Philip, but I would say about that building he's doing for AT&T: it's fine to have the broken pediment on top, but how about the cabriole legs on the bottom to complete it? But I think that one can't jump at conclusions. One has to see the talent and brilliance in everything that's coming. And this is an amazing period. The Modern movement was dead-ended after Le Corbusier. It wasn't developing and fulfilling itself in organic richness. So there's been a search for something; and I think the trouble has been that people then went backwards—even Gropius started to warm up his stuff, which I felt was very bad, because it wasn't continuous. It was almost giving up the strong philosophy that he'd started with and then faltering; it's like a plane stalling in mid-air and dropping down.

STREATFIELD: Well, it's interesting that you brought up Post Modernism, because this morning as I was looking at your work and listening to you talk, the thought was going through my mind that you were really Post-Modern years before this movement appeared. It seems to me that's exactly what you've done in your work.

KILEY: Yes, well, I love Le Nôtre, and all his work. I felt that he was doing things spatially then, only in a formal, symmetrical way that I feel are important today. And that's why the continuity is easy when you link up with that. On my first job, in 1940, the Charles Collier project, I used every cliché in the book. It had wiggles and curves and sawtooths and everything. But it didn't take me too long to shake off that stuff from the California school and other modernistic styles–diamonds and kidneys, and all that sort of thing. You get them out of your system and start to look at the problem straight. Even if it happens to be only a straight line, and it curves slightly, you're looking for a diagram that is saying what this particular thing is about, because it's about life. All the early things called "art" that we have in the museums were living things that people used–they made the amphorae for serving wine or oil. But we put them in museums now as works of art–even guns, all decorated up beautifully. I still feel there's no such thing as pure art, abstracted from life. If you took the religion out of Giotto, you wouldn't have anything there. The Gothic cathedral, to me, was the last summation of the essence of pure architecture, done, not by architects, but by master builders and master craftsmen, doing this thing as a total system. Frank Lloyd Wright said that, and after that it turned into a Mannerist kind of selectivity– you can do this here, that there, this there–an eclectic selection of materials. I think when people have to be amused and it's fashionable, that's when the whole thing comes apart. If you do that in architecture and landscape architecture, you're in the fashion business, doing the latest idea that titillates, and it's not that serious. Like some people are now making gardens with bagels– I like to eat them, but…I feel there's not a thing called an art form that you impose upon the land. The art form should be growing out of the whole of nature and man–that's where the art should be coming from. And this is a higher possibility that reaches up and engages all of man's poetry and thought.

STREATFIELD: Another thing that you mentioned this morning which intrigued me a great deal was the notion of appropriateness. We have seen dramatic contrasts between some of the early things you showed us, your house at Wing's Point, for example, and the Oakland Museum and some of the much more formal projects in urban areas. Yet, it seemed to me that everything you showed us was really a very appropriate response to a specific place and time and to either an individual client or group of people. Incidentally, I remember that when I visited Wing's Point years ago in the early sixties I was chatting with some people who lived in Charlotte, and they said, "Oh, you're going to see Dan Kiley, are you? He's a very strange man, you know. He has this great reputation—he's considered to be one of the best landscape architects in the country—and yet you should see that place he lives on: he hasn't done anything to it. It looks like a run-down farm. It's not at all the sort of place you would associate with a landscape architect." But when I got to your farm, I thought, "My God, those people don't understand anything! This place is so beautiful, and so right." I don't know whether you did do anything there, but it had a quality of inevitability. The concept of appropriateness seems to me to be a very important component of design, certainly for architects and landscape architects. What I want to ask is whether this concept was something that developed over the years or was it something that you took cognizance of at an early point in your career?

KILEY: I didn't take cognizance of it in the early part, but I do very much now. I think the basic problem with a lot of designs, like the cities I mentioned, is that they're in the wrong place. It all depends on the rightness of that first diagram—a structure that works, like the human body—fingernails are like Zen gardens, right? But if that diagram isn't correct, appropriate to the situation, then nothing will work afterwards. You can jazz it up and "design" it and over design it, but you never make it, because it's basically wrong to start with. It think that appropriateness is very important. But it has nothing to do with cost. I like to say Americans can take gold and make it vulgar. Some of the Europeans and others can too. But consider the lovely promenade in almost every little French town—a grove of plane trees planted in a sand-clay mixture. The cost of the sand-clay is just about nothing. The cost of the paving that Americans think they need to walk on is anywhere from $10 to $50 a square foot. When we start to talk to clients, they say, "I want to keep it simple—to save money here to put the money somewhere else." But when we suggest clay or something besides paving, they say, "Oh, well, maintenance would be a problem, and we would track in dirt, and people can't walk on it in high heels." Every time I've been to Vaux-le-Vicomte and walked a half mile or more down the walk, the only people ahead of me are American women with high heels, who are walking on this crushed rock. Incidentally, I think the part that isn't maintained, where they don't rake up the leaves, is much more beautiful than the part that is maintained. The part that's maintained is kind of cold and sterile; but where the leaf mixture is in with the rocks, it's very beautiful, warm, and rich.

So appropriateness is a key thing, putting the right thing in the right place. It's just like an airplane, you know, with a wing on each side, or a bird—I mean, the bird is appropriate. All natural things are. The tree is beautiful because its whole structural system is working for it. And it's doing its thing in nature, what it has to do.

I remember Ian McHarg called me down to the University of Pennsylvania in the very early days when he was just getting started. The students were working on a little ecological problem. I don't know whether you were there, David, but a lot of your friends were. They had a little area to work on, and they were making all these little ecological scenes, with groupings of plant

STREATFIELD: This morning you talked about Le Nôtre and "the poetry of space," which I think is a marvelous phrase. Now I'm wondering if there are not times when the appropriate design is more the kind of loose, naturalistic landscapes of Capability Brown and Humphry Repton. In certain circumstances, aren't those appropriate special solutions, where one could create a situation which is indeed poetic in spatial terms?

material, and I said, "You've seen the site—what are you doing? Here's what the site says: pitch pine, *Pinus rigida*, and a groundcover of *Cornus stolonifera*. And that's all in that whole site." I said, "How can you put in all these different little associations? You can't make a model of the environment. It has to be it—real." So that kind of shattered everybody for a while. The other thing I hate is principles—rules, questions and answers, all tied up in ribbon. That's what most people want—they want the answers. But thought is born of failure. Once you fail, you start to think. And that's the point of departure.

KILEY: That's another good question... You know, in England, which doesn't have the American wilderness, there's probably a need for some kind of condition approximating nature, somewhere. The thing that I have against Capability Brown—and I'd shoot him right now (I have no problems about conviction)—is that he just went ahead and destroyed so much beauty in England, great classic gardens and beautiful terraces and walls, in one swoop. He said, "You jump the wall and all England's a garden." But, as I started out by saying, I believe man is nature, and his civilized cultural imprint is as important as the print of the trees and the fields and the geese. I'm not against having loose landscapes, but first you have to have architecture of the space out-side. And it is architecture. The Italian villa is the great example, where the villa and the terraces are all archi-tecture—a unified whole. But then nature laps against the edge of it. And so you have the whole thing. You're not just having what Capability Brown did at Harewood House, for instance. On one side was just a park where you come in, and a beautiful big lawn approaching the front door. That's fine. But then on the other side there were classical terraces that went down, and then there was a meadow, and pond, and so forth. Well, Capability Brown ripped out the classical terraces. And Robert Adam was a bad boy, too, at Harewood House. Although a fine architect, he ripped away all the columns in front, destroying the kind of great shade and shadow and beautiful detail that Jefferson was trying to import to this country. He swept it all out and made it a flat facade.

Now exactly the same thing happens with mis-guided people in America. I'm thinking now of my own town, Charlotte. There are a lot of colonial houses there that happen to be oriented to the west, and the hot sun came in. So around 1880 or the early 1900s they added porches, and they really worked, and they were beautiful. I've seen more of these porches ripped

LAURIE OLIN: Dan's thoughts are like rabbits—they just keep leaping out. I hardly know where to begin. When I was in my third year of architecture school at the University of Washington, a strange man with blue eyes arrived; he was a landscape architect, and nobody knew what to do with him, so they stuck him in our studio. His name was Rich Haag. I didn't know anything about landscape architecture. I'd certainly never heard of Dan Kiley. I don't think I'd even heard of Olmsted—perhaps because I grew up in Alaska. Well, very odd things began to happen in the studio: one of the results was that within a few years most of the top students in architecture ended up working for Rich Haag. He was a very interesting, forceful personality—he kept rabbits in the backyard, he had six or eight kids, and he had this sort of spaced-out attitude toward things, and he was always telling us to slow down. If we wanted to start work on a site, he'd tell us we should go out and sleep on it— wake up in the morning there. What he was telling us seemed counter to the hybrid education we were getting, which was Beaux-Arts meets Harvard-post-Gropius. It was a very strange time. And then here comes this person with mud on his shoes, talking about Zen masters and asking if we had ever really been in an aspen grove, and he'd start wiggling and jiggling. And I can tell you, during the last two days I have thought, "Aha! Rich Haag worked for Dan Kiley for a while!" And as a matter of fact there is a direct personal relationship between people who teach and their students and practitioners and those who work for them. It's very interesting to discover that, like myself, Dan Kiley doesn't have a degree in landscape architecture, and is a certain kind of Yankee autodidact. But there are personal relationships that tie him to other traditions, and I find that very interesting. He talked about Manning this morning; and one of the things that intrigues me, Dan, is to know a little bit more about what you did with Manning, some of the things you worked on. But clearly there's a lot more to your own self-development than either Harvard or Manning.

off, and then you find a house sitting eight feet above grade, without the porch, and the sun is beating down on it, and they think they're being "Colonial." Most people who think they want a Colonial house don't want one at all. You can't make an exact copy of anything from the past because the things you do are not Colonial: your heating, your electricity, your kitchen, your lack of servants, the craftsmanship, the materials available, everything! There's nothing that you can make Colonial anymore. And yet these people love Colonial. My wife's family had a beautiful house in Greenfield Hill, Connecticut, 1770 something–such a lovely house you couldn't believe it. They finally had to sell it–they moved out because they realized that New York was creeping up on them, so they moved up to where we were, in Vermont. The people that bought it loved Colonial, and it still distresses me to see what they did to the house–they just ruined the whole beautiful thing that was there.

There are some other threads there; and I'd be curious to know what you think were some of the other things that helped. Because clearly your work went through some kind of transformation based on other influences.

KILEY: That's also a good question. I was brought up in the heart of Boston, where there are backyards and alleys—you get this mix of wonderful architecture—the basis of the city. And I'd climb over fences and run through alleys, and so forth. Then, every summer I went up to my grandmother Baxter's in New Hampshire. She had a little upland farm. She ran through four husbands, and she ended up jumping over a puddle when she was 97, when I was walking with her. I spent the whole summer on this beautiful little farm. It was a complete contrast to the city. Hers was the oldest house in the town; it was one of those low New Hampshire houses that hugged a rocky little ridge. And then you walked down from there, through the barnyard and out into a field, and there were flat rocks, and the hot smell of juniper and pine, and then you'd go into the pine woods. And this experience combined with the other was almost the strongest sensation that I had—it was architecture and nature together, you might say. And, although I didn't know anything about architecture, it hit me very strongly. And I think that's probably the big reason I got interested in both nature and the city. (And, besides, my middle name is Urban.)

Manning's office is, in effect, a seedbed. Manning wasn't a great designer in the physical sense at all. He was a very enthusiastic thinker and influential in getting parks, as I said earlier. In his office, though, he had people working, like Charles Gillette and A. D. Taylor, and the best one was Fletcher Steele, who did beautiful drawings, which inspired me very much. One man who worked for Manning had gotten the Charles Eliot Prize to travel and study for a year. His name was Sylvester, and he introduced me to the techniques of drawing. We used to visit Fletcher Steele's office. I was inspired by these beautifully-done drawings—beautiful things in themselves, but also communicating instruments. Making such drawings is a creative act in itself, which can sustain a draftsman working in an office, even though he doesn't design a thing. But in Manning's office, I remember, I worked for nothing, and then after a year I got fifty cents an hour. This was the Depression, you know. And we worked on some WPA projects, since nobody had work. One of them was to look at the islands in Boston Harbor and see how to stop the erosion and also make them beautiful. And Manning was like the old man of the sea. There was an historian named Edward Grove Snow who took us around in a motorboat to all the

OLIN: It answers the questions one doesn't need to ask. I dug out an old 1940 article, one of a series of three, I guess, that you did with Rose and Eckbo. I was fascinated to read it, and I'd like to recommend the students read it, because it's rather an eye-opener to discover that in 1940, with the war going on, these people are writing a little article saying we're going to have a big problem with open space, having to do with changes in lifestyle. It's a whole discussion of the wilderness, with words like "ecological," and issues that I thought were first raised in my period. And you realize someone was there already and worrying about those things, but nobody was listening, apparently. Yet it intrigued me this morning that you said you are not all that taken by planners with their checklists, and yet what a lot of people like Ian McHarg have tried to do is keep people from building Calgary in the wrong place. Ian was trying to make the world safe for fools, I think. So that there was this fool-proof "cookbook" that you could follow. So I'm wondering how you relate to the people dealing with environmental problems? And what happened to these articles and your attitudes expressed in them?

islands. He'd have to carry Manning through the water on his back—this old man with a white beard. Another beautiful thing about Manning was that he was so unself-conscious. I remember him talking to an architect named Clark who used an ear trumpet. The trumpet didn't bother Manning at all, and he was talking so enthusiastically he started spitting into it. I can't hear so well myself, and one of the fringe benefits of that job at Gallaudet College was to receive all the latest electronic tests and hearing equipment. They ended up telling me, "You're right on the borderline; you don't really need it." I said "Give me the trumpet anyway." I have to sit close, especially to blondes, very close. I don't know if that answers your question...

KILEY: It was Jim Fitch—James Marsten Fitch—who came to us and suggested writing these three articles. The first one was on the urban environment—landscape design in the urban environment. The second one was on the rural environment; this one, the third, was on the primeval environment. I must say that Jim and Garrett did most of the writing. I didn't do much of it. We worked together and everything, and exchanged thoughts, but they could handle this better than I could. I'd just like to read one part here, where we quote from Lewis Mumford, who was a great source. He was one of the greatest men in that period, who looked at and understood the total problem. "As Lewis Mumford points out," we said, "the purpose is 'to make the region ready to sustain the richest types of human culture and the fullest span of human life—offering a home to every type of character and disposition and human mood, creating and preserving objective fields of response for man's deeper subjective needs. It is precisely those of us who recognize the value of mechanization and standardization and universalization who must be most alert to the need for providing an equal place for the complementary set of activities…the natural as opposed to the human… the lonely as opposed to the collective. A habitat planned so as to form a continuous background to a delicately graded scale of human feelings and value is a genuine requisite of a cultivated life.'"[1]

OLIN: One of the things that interests me in looking at your work is the misunderstanding of words like "formal" and "informal." It's clear that a lot of people use "informal" when they mean forms other than Euclidean geometry. It seems to me the geometries of your work are very misunderstood. An important part of the Beaux-Arts tradition, of course, was the work of Vignola—in which there's an absolute interrelationship between buildings and landscape. The two are inextricable—you can't say what is the landscape and what is the building, because it's all of one piece. And bilateral symmetry became part of the rule of how to do that. And it's very clear in looking at Dan's work that there are axial relationships, there are symmetries, there are bilaterally symmetrical elements. Yet, in project after project it's very clear that there is a strong change. Part of what we think of as modern in the work is clearly that you're doing something different with the relationships of the formal geometry. I have some idea what they are, and I think we could diagram some of them. But what I'm curious about, Dan, is what you thought you were doing when you did these things. How are they different from the Beaux-Arts formal? What are the differences in the relationships that you feel you can talk about?

KILEY: Well, I think that's what modern design is all about. And again, appropriateness comes in. Sometimes, it's appropriate to have a symmetrical scheme, I mean you shouldn't avoid it–you shouldn't avoid what is. If that's the problem and the function of the space, then you're not going to deliberately make it asymmetrical. What I think has excited me and excites me now is that poetry of space, where space is continuous; where two-dimensional space gets broken down into a movement–dynamic movement that never ends, but extends to infinity. Movement that is ever continuous and elusive, like a maze. It's like a mystery. It's a mystic quality of space developed by the structural means that you have such as trees and other things. It's just like modern architecture, which broke down the plan. Frank Lloyd Wright, and before that the Victorians, had broken down tight symmetrical compartments into a flowing of space. We are getting back now to compartments, especially in buildings where you have dining rooms and separate rooms enclosed. But the reason originally for the open plan was partly cost; you could get more for your money by having a multiple use of spaces, like living/dining. And gardens and the landscape were reaching to embrace the land around you and have it as part of you, free, in effect.

Jefferson's Lawn here at the University of Virginia got closed by the small thinking of McKim, Meade, and

White, by putting a building at the end, which is below the ground level as you look across it; no Beaux-Arts designer would ever accept that as a decent solution, to have the ground plane cut the columns in half. Besides that, it stopped the movement out into nature that Jefferson wanted—a continuous thing that went forever. His design was perfect. It should never have been closed. Even in those days Jefferson had realized he was doing spatial continuity, and Le Nôtre, too, had done it. I think that is the essence of what I am interested in and excited about; I like the open movement and a change and continuity in some mystic impulse. The genetic catching of infinity is what Einstein is talking about, and it's the universe itself which is expanding and contracting, it is always going. I think that's the main difference in design today—or could be, but not many people have jumped on to that. Instead they jump on to little scenes, like little circles and kidneys and diamonds and little two-dimensional things on the ground. They can be important as related to the large scheme, but they have to be organic with it, just like the fingernail is organic with the finger and the leg bone is connected with the ham bone and all that sort of thing. Design concerns shouldn't be arbitrary or whimsical. They should be rich extenuations and fulfillments of the structure itself. I think that our understanding of the universe is what makes landscape design today a moving, dynamic, exciting thing. My whole idea in the Third Block of Independence Mall was to set up a dynamism of this architectural grove so every step you take the trees' faces change and they keep moving, like a Vasarely painting. And the painters are doing that too. You're trying to get a vibration. That Agam's sculpture with paving was that way too. I feel that I haven't exploited it or gotten into it; I don't know enough about it as an artist to even develop it more than that. It's just the start of a development.

OLIN: Can we push this just a little further? Take the Miller House. There are always things other people have done that you wish you had thought of. You did something in that project which is rather interesting to me, and that is one of the simplest, strongest elements in the project: the allée of honey-locusts in the gravel in the front. It's absolutely at right angles to the way the space is really moving, and so there is a certain contradiction built in. It is an element that seems to come from nowhere and go nowhere, and you blunder through it, and then you discover it does something else important. Meanwhile, the whole landscape is going down to the water and there's this rather romantic, lush, park-like place at the other end. So you really offer the alternative, although you seem to be saying, "You know, we don't do that"—but there you did it.

KILEY: Oh no, we do it when it's appropriate, apt. I mean, down there by the water it wouldn't have been appropriate to do geometry at all because of the physical conditions, with the possibility of water coming in via the stream and the woods; these called for that response. And it is, you might say, amusing, you know, a little added amusement. The house I compare to the Villa

Rotunda in the fact that it's a separate temple on a podium. And, just like at the Villa Rotunda you can't start extending lines from the complex outwardly; you have to do it in the round, in effect. So in this case the axis across is functional, and because the ground drops off there and you went into the meadow, the effect of a balustrade of big trees was created. It was really a balustrade of trunks. It also provided protection from the hot western sun, engaged it, and gave it that kind of continuity. And that was the first job where I had the chance to try to achieve dynamic spatial movement, by way of grove, orchard, line, and materials; and I think it's the best thing I've ever done, and they keep it beautifully.

PORTER: Now let's have questions from the audience.

QUESTION: You've never written a book, you've never been a department head. The names that I associate with success are Sasaki and Gropius, who at one time or another were active in the profession as department heads, and they wrote. Tell me how you got where you are and how you managed to bypass the usual routes.

KILEY: Well, it's called rolling with nature, or living— having trust in nature and the world, and being optimistic. I'm glad I never wrote anything, because it would have been dumb as hell. And I think most of what was written is pretty boring. I mean, to start to write before you've done anything is very dangerous. Over ten years ago, Harper and Row asked me to write a book. And I started to try to do something on it, and then they had a big upheaval in Harper and Row. The editor I was working with went to Houghton Mifflin, so that sort of got cut off. Now, though, we keep saying, "What we really need is a brochure in the office." Because every single time we have to make a presentation, it's always an original thing, digging up photographs, and trying to get them together. But recently a Japanese magazine, *Process*, has been preparing an issue on my work, which will be our first brochure, and may be the basis for some kind of book. It's just showing works, rather than a lot of rhetoric.

When I first set up, after leaving Washington, D.C., in 1941, I moved to Sugar Hill, in Franconia, New Hampshire. I didn't have any work up there at all, although I had a couple of jobs still in Washington. Since there was no landscape work, by default I became an architect. Being over-optimistic and dumb, I decided I'd design buildings. I mean, if the Architect's Collaborative could do it, why couldn't I? And do it better? I'd just gotten back from the Nuremberg trials, which I designed in Germany for the war trials, and it was late in December. Since I had no work, I wanted to ski. My wife and I both became certified ski instructors and taught that year. She was a much better skier than I. It was very exciting and pretty fancy to be a ski instructor. You had your badge, and you go into the bar afterwards and have a few drinks and meet people. And I met a client that way who wanted a house built. And so I did his house. Aldo Giurgola was running *Interiors* magazine then, and he published the house. And out of that I started getting houses–lots of houses, no landscapes– until Eero Saarinen finally wrote and asked if I would like to join in on the Jefferson Memorial Competition in St. Louis. And then I got work through old friends, like Lou Kahn, Eero Saarinen, Harry Weese, and all those people. There was no competition because I was the only one available on the East Coast who thought like they did architecturally. It was easy. And now, if I had an office in New York, it would be twice as big as Sasaki's, without question. But I only get the jobs that are willing to come up that far north and pay expenses –and I charge more than anyone else in the country. As a matter of fact, when things get rough and I don't have enough work, I raise my fee.

It's a personal thing really. You just jump into things. You're optimistic. I never feel negative about myself. I'm ready to take on anything, go out on a limb, to risk failure. One shouldn't worry about failing. Americans were brought up to think that they can't fail. Why not? With the Zen approach, failure doesn't even come into the vocabulary. Some people are always seeking rules by which to do things. I think a lot of the problem with schools is that they introduce you to a way of perform- ing by way of rules. And there aren't any. My rules are openmindedness, if possible, tabula rasa–the client has an open pocketbook–open time schedules, proper drinking and eating. Lots of times I arrive at a project after missing the whole morning meeting, and I say, "Gosh, I'm glad I made it for lunch!" People say, "Now, we don't have time; we have to bring some sandwiches in." I tell them I work twice as fast and much better when I'm properly fed and when I drink properly. Then I'm with the universe–I'm with nature. I'm not like a Madison Avenue type pounding out a living and trying to squeeze out everything he can. Eero Saarinen, whom I loved, was a great genius, but the difference between him and Alvar Aalto, who was the greater architect, I must say, was that Eero was always working. I lived with him for four months on that Jefferson project, and we never had one second off. He was always talking about the design and drawing–at lunch. He drew a cartoon of me looking sad...my eyebrows go down like this…because I'm sorry for myself because I'm listening to talk about work when I want to drink and have fun. And they claim Aalto didn't even have a telephone.

I think the big thing is not getting up tight about things and loosening up. As I say, I got my greatest inspiration reading wonderful people. Other artists have inspired me too. Like painters who say something very damn good. You can't get enough of looking. You can't get enough of seeing what's been done in the past. Looking at the present. Looking at good and bad all the time. You're interested in, say, a drip cap, even though you're a landscape architect. You're interested in how a thing works and how it would work better and why it is that way. It's curiosity. Like Thomas Jefferson had. He was amazing. His curiosity spread over all fields. I think that's what it is.

QUESTION: I'd like to know if you have been to some special places that influenced your thinking.

KILEY: Yes, many. All places influence my thinking. For a while I didn't want to go to Japan because Europe was enough, and I hadn't seen enough there. Although when I was at Harvard, before Gropius came and there was nothing but the Beaux-Arts, I had turned to the Orient. I used to sign my name *Ki-lee* with a Japanese brush on rice paper. All my scenes had moon gates and all kinds of things like that. But every place you go is terribly exciting and inspiring. I can't get enough of the chateaus, for instance. I've seen many of them, but I'm still eager to see more and more because they tell you so much. They're so rich, and they can be anywhere, not just in Europe. We went, at lunch, to see the Farmington place that Jefferson did, which was a marvelous thing to see right here. The landscape impressed me very much, because all he used was boxwood around the whole place and nothing else. Very simple and unified. There's a great lesson there: not to throw a lot of things around. You simply go with something and relate it. But, you know, of every place in the world—England, France, Italy, Japan, etc.–I think America has the best current landscape architecture. The early Japanese gardens were marvelous, but there are no modern landscape architects there. But I should point out that Americans think all Japanese design is the little Zen garden. Actually every Zen garden has a real frame, an architectural frame around it. It's not a loose thing. It usually has a white wall with a coping, or a clipped hedge making a frame. And then inside is a scene. It's like a painting or a sculpture. But the organization of other spaces in Japan, like the palaces and temples, are very French– or very Japanese, I mean. A big temple and a very big symmetrical courtyard. Big scale. Crushed rock and two

QUESTION: You seem to be talking about your approach to landscape architecture as one which is in tune with the times and in tune with the expression of man and his life at any particular time, rather than recreating the past, for example. Where do you see the influences in landscape architecture now and in the next ten years in light of changes in society from the highly organized technological attitudes we've had to a time of diminishing resources and economic concerns?

trees, or one tree, and that's it. What inspired me in Japan, as I've said before, were not the gardens but the houses—the way the houses are organized by the module and beautiful textural quality. In Korea, too.

KILEY: From my point of view, the approach is exactly the same. It's just that conditions are different, and you have new problems with new conditions. However, there's no difference in the approach. It's like something the Japanese magazine was asking: "What is your approach to the residence, to the corporation, to the public scene?" I said, "There's no difference in approach. It's exactly the same, except that the conditions are different, the requirements are different." So it is really the same process. In the future, you just have to keep up with the times, you have to read, and see what's happening. You're bombarded by television, of course. There's so much stuff that you can't see what's really happening. All through history, the Greeks and everybody had the same approach. Only their problems were different, the society was different. Take the use of columns. That has spatial excitement just like modern tree arrangements. Whether you have a job that costs ten dollars or one that costs a million, it's still the same approach. Where do you put the trees? What do you do with this material? It's still the same.

I think that there are certain people that are dedicated to improving the social condition of man, which is very laudatory. And there are a lot of architects, especially in Europe, who are radicals who are working to change the system. I feel the danger in that is that the talent to create or design things is one kind of talent, and the talent to organize communes and social conditions and communities is a different kind of talent. Now, both might occur in the same person, but often they don't.

QUESTION: Mr. Kiley, you became interested in design rather than something else. When did you recognize that you had a special talent for it?

KILEY: I recognize I have talent in many fields, but I used to think I had more talent. The younger I was, the more talent I thought I had. That's the trouble with the young. The older you get, the more you realize you're not that good in anything you do. You get a little more humble each year. I just had a feeling that I loved to do this sort of thing. It's a love. I think you have to do what you love. Doing something you don't love is a waste of time. I happen to love what I do. I get a little annoyed by

the planning process, especially the collection of data.
Most planners think the collection of data is planning.
It isn't at all. They collect too much data, usually the
wrong data, and then after they get the data they make
the wrong decisions because they're not in tune enough
with the whole. I'm not saying all planners are this way.
I'd say 90 percent are. I started to do buildings because I
was impatient. I wanted to see something built. Landscape
takes a long time. I didn't take the advice of lots of
friends and other people who said, "Just stick to landscape architecture. That's what you are." I still wanted to
do buildings, here and there, just to show, "Gee, I can
do third-rate architecture as well as the next architect."
I didn't ever dream I could be on the top at all. Third
is pretty damn high. Maybe I'm being too generous.
Fourth, let's call it fourth. But 90 percent of the people
are at the fourth level, and then it thins out. At the top
you have very few people. You have Robertson, you have
Pei, and a few other people, but not many. Sometimes we
get jobs before an architect has been chosen, and we call
the architects in. We try to think of lists of architects.
And when you get down to it, we can seldom think of
even five. We can't find an architect who could really do
that job. We go through that process all the time trying
to find the right architect for certain conditions. It's not
easy. There are very, very few in the world. There may
be young people who are wonderful. But they are in
different offices, and may not have the stuff to make it
on their own. Still, there are very talented designers all
over the place.

QUESTION: Would you say the same thing about
landscape architecture?

KILEY: Definitely. I don't think more than three or
four are really doing things that help.

QUESTION: Who are they?

KILEY: Well, I think Sasaki, naturally. They've done a
hell of a lot of work. Sasaki has a big organization, and he
gets lost in the business. He's finally retired. And Larry
Halprin I have respect for. He's done some very nice
things. I like him anyway. He came to my lecture in
Berkeley. So did Sasaki and Garrett Eckbo and Bob
Royston. My title was "Works of Dan Kiley." But when
I saw this impressive audience, I changed the title to
"Advice to Young Students and All Others Who Aren't
Geniuses." The title of a talk is important. It can make or
break it. And then Bob Zion is, in certain things, very
good. I guess that's about it.

QUESTION: Are there any Europeans who are doing
good work?

KILEY: Yes. I think the ones that are doing the best
work are the Germans and the Swiss. The Swiss always
had a beautiful sense of scale and design—especially in
paving. As a matter of fact, we're working on a 27-million-

dollar park in New York City on the Hudson River between 59th and 72nd streets, and when we made a presentation before the Park and City Planning commissions and the community, instead of showing my work I showed the Zurich Park in Switzerland. It's a beautiful design, and I was comparing it to possibilities in New York. I took them along the promenades in Zurich, showing them the groves and the big sweep of grass. There is a beautiful flat lawn with very few flowers, but the flowers are geometrically arranged just in the right place. The paving is also beautiful, and then there is Le Corbusier's last building, that colorful little building in one corner. And Henry Moore sculptures happened to be out all through the park when I was there. It changes from being very formal where you hit the crenulated edge of the lake and then you come up onto the lawn and the whole thing moves beautifully. People say I'm hypercritical, that I don't like anybody but myself, but when I see something I like, I really flip, like about that Zurich park. I think it's beautiful, and I don't care who did it.

When I was at the American Academy in Rome, in residence, 1975–76, I took them at their word and didn't do any work. I just took trips all over the place by myself. Once in a while I took some students with me. I went especially through Germany to look at some of the new work they've done, like at Mannheim–very good parks. And Cologne has a very nice plaza with a beautiful, very fresh kind of fountain in it and an arch in concrete. It has beautiful highly glazed tiles of different colors, and water comes out all over the place.

I think Larry Halprin's new job–the little park over the freeway in Seattle–is very nice. He didn't have a chance to get into the spatial thing that I like, but it's still handled well and has nice plant materials. Larry's always great for waterfalls. I disagree with his thinking about nature, though, about the way he wants to take nature and recreate a man's scene out of it. I think that's wrong. As I told you, we are nature.

QUESTION: You said you design intuitively. Could you elaborate?

KILEY: I do both.

QUESTION: How does the intellect condition your intuition?

KILEY: Oh, I'd have to ask Carl Jung that. We haven't spoken yet of the physical conditioning of a person, how it affects his whole attitude and approach. That's very important. I happen to have a not very big intellect. I'm interested in the thought of different people, but I'm not a scholar. I like to use my mind as much as I can. I use my intuition. I use my body and my faith. You might say I try to connect with the spirit of all those things that are important. And, like I said, the best time of my life was really educating myself, because I didn't go to college. In the early days, when I couldn't afford to fly, I used to take the train from Boston all the way out to the West Coast and back. I'd jump off at Peoria or that place where they make the tractors in Illinois and put a plan in the mailbox. By the time I got to the West Coast I had four plans done, all sent back. I had a chance to really read then. I read as much philosophy as I could. I'd get very excited, especially by Goethe, Henry James, Jefferson, and Kierkegaard. Heraclitus is the one that excites me the most. He's a blast—a gas! His theory is that the universe is in flux and it's floating; it's only gas anyway. I feel that one should start on a problem with a tabula rasa, a clean slate. This is impossible, of course, but one should start with as few preconceptions as possible. Try to get the work, the impact, coming from the people. The interchange of people is very important. I don't believe in saying, "I'm a genius. I'm going to make a design for society." I like to get the design growing up the other way with interchange all the way through. Whether it's a single client or a community. I did a job in Seattle for Fort Lawton, and we had a public meeting with 36 different community organizations before we even started to design. And I got up and explained the basic conditions and talked about them and said, "This is the area. This is it." I wanted to elicit some direction from them. And the next time we came, we had a very, very rough schematic plan. And I talked about it and got interchange. We had six meetings with 36 different organizations. At the end, the design was unanimously approved because they were all part of it.

QUESTION: You talked a lot about inspiration and learning from the past, and you mentioned that Le Nôtre was one of the people who influenced you. I was wondering what were some of the specific things that you saw in Le Nôtre's work that you really admired and that influenced you, and how did they take form in your work?

KILEY: Well, all of it. For example, the Tuileries, with horse chestnuts ten feet on center each way. When Frederick Law Olmsted, Sr., saw that, he thought it was the most beautiful place in the world. The American Society of Landscape Architects doesn't even know he said that. Well, if they did, they'd probably hide it because it destroys all their naturalistic ideas. Even though it's symmetrical design, these masses of trees are doing something else for this design. Remember those groves of trees at Vaux-le-Vicomte? They're encompassing. They're enframing other aspects and they're working all the way through as design elements. They're not just whimsical. They're not just an idea: I want to make a grove. A grove is working as a part, an integral part, of the whole design and that's a great thing.

A theory I have that relates to Le Nôtre is that one reason the great masters in painting and sculpture and other arts were great is that when they did their work they were connected with their universe in their time. And they solved their problems in that relationship. It's that fact that makes them stay with us. We look at the Old Masters even with the eyes of today and appreciate them. For instance, the boulevards that Le Nôtre laid out were for shooting cannonballs down–that's what boulevard means, you see. But then it changed into avenue, which means a coming. In our day it's an avenue because it's a gracious movement from someplace. But it was for defense before. And Versailles acts as the most public park that you can find anywhere, even though it was designed for a king. It still works in another function better than almost any park I know. Rather than the kind of mediocrity of little cute scenes. One other thing is that the large structure of the design is the important thing. The big development, the big structure is everything. Forget the little design. You know, they're things that both strengthen and fulfill the large structure, but they should be of the nature of it, too, because it's continuity and unity and is becoming, just like any organic thing–like a bird, or an animal, or you. A perfect example of design is the human body. It's all there. All this detail and complication. And a mystery, too.

QUESTION: You mentioned the role of the artist and the role of the craftsman. Can you talk a little about how you see yourself as a designer between those two roles?

KILEY: I suspect "artist" in quotation marks. There are an awful lot of people who call themselves artists and, again, like architects, there are very few who really are. The craftsman is now in a different position than he was in history. Then he was a functional, integral part of society, providing things for people. Now he's in "art," and I don't like that. Very few people in all those movements as far as I've seen are producing very much. I've seen a lot of potters, and their pots are mediocre. If you've seen one pot from a real primitive society, it's so far superior... I saw the exhibition of the development of Korean pottery, and it was just amazing. To distinguish it, the crafts movement is one thing, but then there are artists who are outside the crafts movement. Just like I'm outside the American Society of Landscape Architects. I mean, why should I join. I don't get insurance. I hate saying "the profession of landscape architecture." To hell with the profession. The art is the important thing in landscape design, not the profession. But I did more single-handedly to raise the fee schedule in the government than the American Society of Landscape Architects. When Harry Weese asked me to do a housing project, their fee was 6 percent. I said, "Well, my fee is 7 percent."

QUESTION: Here at the University, it is accepted as an article of faith that the Lawn and the historic buildings here are the best architecture and environmental design in the United States. In fact, the Jefferson design won an award from the American Institute of Architects two years ago. Do you agree with that, and if so, why do you think it is so exceptional?

So I wouldn't do the job unless I got 7 percent, which they paid in that case. They had been lobbying to get the fees raised and raised. Again, it's an individual thing which you do on your own. Organizations, I think, are very suspect–crafts or architectural or whatever organizations. They become places where people that aren't producing on their own become important. You know, the talkers and the organizers who administer the meetings.

KILEY: I do agree completely. As I said, Jefferson was a beautiful, broad man in every area. He did more for the country and the world than almost anybody else–even in a period of quite a few great men like that. The reason I think the Lawn is so beautiful–although you can't describe proportion that well–is you have the beautiful Rotunda at the head and the two lines of ranges going down and dropping down like this. And, of course, Jefferson wanted it to continue out into space, which it should. But McKim, Meade, and White put the building at the end, so when you're up here and you look at it, the columns are cut in two. The other thing is, if that building weren't here, there would be a beautiful magic about that space as it goes down. It's ineffable. It's something you can't grasp. And that is true about good design in any area, in any field. It has a quality like a miracle. Take any Frank Lloyd Wright plan; just look at the plan. You know it works. It's beautiful. How you describe it is another thing. It's all the old rules of the past, but another person can't take these rules and produce such a plan. I have a theory that if you want an old building restored, or added to, you don't go to an architect specializing in restoring. You go to the best architect in the world, who will be a modern architect, and have him do it, because he's sensitive, he understands and respects proportion, scale, and detail.

What makes the Lawn exquisite is that there's an organic totality there on that site, and it's wonderful. It's impossible to describe it more. It's just apt. It has taste. It has elegance. It has a beautiful understanding of the site. I'd give it another award.

JAQUELIN ROBERTSON: I have two or three observations on which you may or may not wish to comment. First, you mentioned you were asked to work with Saarinen and others because you were the only one who understood what they did. I feel you understood the invisible connection between buildings and the land on which they sat, which, unfortunately in the twentieth century came apart. You understood the relationship between building and garden—the essential glue which is landscape architecture. In fact, I think that all of the buildings you've shown us today, if stripped of the landscape, would be very minor buildings. You represent the piece which has been missing in modern architecture of wedding building to site, and not seeing them as different activities.

Second, you've shown us the informal way in which you live and examples of your work, which is formal in a certain sense. You know both the city and the country, and you can only know each if you know the other. There is this notion of division, and yet you impose urban order in certain suburban situations and vice versa, I suspect. And that deep love of both city and country is central.

Third, I consider you essentially an urban designer. Since planners have abandoned that role and architects were not trained as such until quite recently, will landscape architects fill the breach? Is that something you think is central to your task—to work and restructure cities, today, to give shape to them?

KILEY: I'll try to answer the last question, since that's the one I remember. I hate the frenzied grabbing of professions for turf. Like the landscape architects–you see it in their magazine all the time: "That should be our job. As landscape architects, we should be planning this; we should be doing that." Forget it! The person who plans it is the person who gets the job, however he gets it. I like to have the opportunity to work with an urban team and do so-called urban planning. A lot of my work involves that. I'd like opportunities to do more of it. And I haven't because I haven't really been selling my services around the country the way bigger firms do. I just take what happens to come along.

The other thing about the design of very urban spaces, whether in an urban, suburban, or rural area, is that you don't have that much space. Take the Hamilton backyard. You couldn't create the sensation of nature there even if you wanted to. That's what it was when we went in there. They had a whole bunch of curlicues –a real mess in there. When you organize space in this other geometrical, simple way and put a roof over it, you get much more out of that little third of an acre than you would if you put a loose row, a woodland kind of thing. Efficiency of space makes it imperative that you organize your spaces that way rather than in a so-called loose way.

What was the first question? Oh, yes. It makes me sound a little egotistical. It sounds like Frank Lloyd Wright. His son wrote that book, *My Father Who is On Earth.* I felt very good being in the position where these architects didn't have anybody else to turn to. There was no competition really. All the other people in the profession were doing just these same things–copying the natural scene. They weren't in sympathy or didn't understand or know the architecture. The fact is that one becomes an architect and thinks in the same spatial terms, trying to integrate building and site, instead of coming in as a gardener and decorating the edges of buildings.

The best architects are better than most of the landscape architects in certain areas because of their design strength. Like I. M. Pei. I would defer in an aesthetic matter because he's a master in that area. And Kevin Roche, too, and you, and other people like that. The only thing is that there is an area that they oversimplify. Like Kevin, now he can plant groves of trees anywhere. But which tree do you use, and does it grow that way or another way, or is it always just a grove of plane trees? There you get into a knowledge of plant materials. A landscape architect must know his materials very, very well, and not skid by. If I didn't know my plant materials, working in London with the contractors there I would look silly. They told me, "*Tilia cordata* (which we specified) isn't a good tree to use here because it's covered with aphids in London, but not in America, and it drops in the groundcover and turns it black." I didn't know this. Then I said, "How about *Tilia euchlora* or *europaea*?" They said, "Yes, both of those are better choices for that."

This is an area in which I think the landscape architect can help even the best architects. Although some architects know all the answers, just like some landscape architects do, especially young ones. The thing that bores me most with young people who come to the office (and they don't last long) is that they think they're little geniuses who know the answers before they study the land or have experience. I say, "If you know the answers … boy, I don't know them, so you better go. Go on your own right away." In the last two years we've had to fire four people with master's degrees because they knew all of the answers, but they couldn't do anything. They were just about helpless, so we were losing money on them right away. I have found that in my office the best way is not to have intermediate designers, but just Peter Ker Walker and myself, and then younger people who are just starting. Some of them are more advanced than others. We've gotten people from the Vermont Technical College who just learned drafting. They work out beautifully, and their pay is a lower scale, and they just produce work. But then, they go on from there. All of them decide to go into architecture or landscape architecture after working for us. At one time we had middlemen who were making almost as much as we were, and they'd be working on a design for weeks, and then we'd have to scrap it and start all over again.

You're spending all that money, you can't afford to. You still have to be clean, crisp businessmen or you won't last. You can't support your office unless you're getting some money to cover your overhead, especially the way I live.

Actually, I live pretty simply compared to conventional people who are as rich as I am. I have big landholdings which are beautiful and protected. We don't have maids. I love to dress well, but I hate to buy new clothes, new suits and all. I like to spend the money on travelling. I like travelling lightly. With me right now I have a very small bag. I've been two weeks in Europe and now here, and I won't get home until Tuesday night. I found I took too many shirts. I took two instead of one. Each night I wash my shirt, my underwear, and my socks. So it's all hot and fresh over the bathtub. But when I'm at home, I have quite a wardrobe of nice things that I like to wear, you know, rather fancy things. I love that. I love dressing. It's just part of my scene. I don't like to be just like an old farmer. I like geometry in the country, too.

1 As quoted in Garrett Eckbo, Daniel U. Kiley, James C. Rose, "Landscape Design in the Primeval Environment," *Architectural Record* (February 1940), p. 77.

/ 1 /

Dan Kiley:
The Nature of Space

Marc Treib

At first glance the Miller garden—constructed to Dan Kiley's design in 1955—appears almost classical in aspect. Almost. The elements that comprise the garden —the allée, the bosque, the orchard, and the lawn—have recurred as basic typologies for almost as long as the designed landscape itself [figure 1-1]. In contrast to the more classical equilibrium and regularity that permeate the various areas of this celebrated residential garden, however, its spatial construction is decidedly modern. Spatial freedom plays against vegetal organization while local symmetries oppose freer overall planning—character-istics of almost all of Kiley's major works, gardens and larger sites alike. It is this handling of space, reinforced by collateral departures from absolute rigidity in the planning geometry, that roots these designs firmly in the twentieth century.

Classical landscape historically centered on the single entity, which in turn governed the form and distribution of the parts. In terms of proportion, prominence, and form, each element was subservient to the whole. At the sixteenth-century Villa Lante in Bagnaia, Italy, for example, the axis descending the hillside at the center of the garden regulates the placement and relations of all the garden's elements: the flights of stairs and statuary, the water course and fountains, and the boxwood-ringed parterres at its base. While Kiley's landscapes certainly possess a sense of entity, they rarely appear as a singular entity immediately comprehended. Moreover, his landscapes rarely rely on the open-ended systems-thinking that elevated process over product during the 1970s and subsequent decades. One witnesses instead, in the course of Kiley's maturation, a freeing of the element within the ensemble, maintaining its own identity while at the same time reinforcing the aggregate. A coherent geometric structure serves as the glue.

In classical landscapes and architecture the global order of the plan and the development of the ground plane,

/ 1-1 /
DAN KILEY,
LANDSCAPE ARCHITECT;
EERO SAARINEN, ARCHITECT;
MILLER GARDEN,
COLUMBUS, INDIANA, 1955.
VIEW TO THE ENTRY OF THE
HOUSE THROUGH THE FRAME
OF THE HORSE CHESTNUT
TREES.
/ MARC TREIB /

understory, and arboreal layers of the section correlate precisely.[1] In contrast, Kiley's landscapes shun any absolute congruence among these stacked layers of landscape elements. Rather than ending neatly at a suggested edge —such as a path or the bed—they overstep their boundaries, merging with one another in a more ambiguous relationship. We might term this property *slippage*: an extension beyond the defined or implied boundary; a purposeful imprecision in aligning elements in plan and in section. What makes this a desirable practice? Discrepancies between the regularity of planting and the openness of the corresponding spaces can enrich our perceptions of the design, particularly its visual readings. For example, a tightly bounded room also circumscribes how the space may be read, while gaps or weakly defined corners allow our view—and perhaps our thoughts—to escape the room, to link with spaces beyond, whether in actuality or solely in our imaginations. Kiley's use of slippage works in just that way: it provokes as well as states.

/ JUXTAPOSITION AND INTERWEAVING /

Regular geometry lies at the base of Kiley's lifelong project. But he did not begin that way. Having passed through Harvard for a year or so in the late 1930s as a special student, Kiley was tinged by the curves and angular geometries evolving into fashionability. A few projects in the 1940s tested his interest in these vocabularies. But soon afterwards, he abandoned the complex interplays of curves and straight lines, circles, and other geometric figures, that qualified the designs of landscape architects such as Thomas Church and Garrett Eckbo in the United States, and Roberto Burle Marx in Brazil.[2] To Kiley, like Le Corbusier, geometry and its rigor were inherent parts of humankind. "Mathematics," claimed the Swiss-French architect, "is the majestic structure conceived by man to grant him comprehension of the universe. It holds both the absolute and the infinite, the understandable and the forever elusive."[3] Employing a related logic, Kiley believed humans—and human talents such as creativity or mathematical prowess—to be a part of nature; by extension, geometry was as well. "Man is nature," Kiley asserted at a symposium on his work in the 1980s. "It's not man *and* nature. It's not man *with* nature. Man *is* nature, just like the trees."[4]

Kiley's philosophical stance resonates in the thinking of the Dutch painter Piet Mondrian, who famously recast existence within an orthogonal structure tinted only by tones of primary hues. In *Natural Reality and Abstract Reality: An Essay in Trialogue Form* Mondrian establishes how the internal world expressed in painting elevates to a higher plane the sensual world of nature. "Everything that appears geometrically in nature shares plastically in the inwardness that is proper to the geometric," he writes. But while "the geometric can manifest itself as either straight or curved, the straight represents the greatest tensing of the curved, which has more of the 'natural'... Many curved lines are discernable in this starry sky, making it still 'natural' and, therefore, demanding intensification to straightness in order to annihilate its naturalness and plastically bring forth its innermost power." He concludes, "Whether in art or simply in conscious contemplation we must reduce the *curved to the straight*."[5] We might posit that in Kiley's use of the straight line and the grid he transforms the seeming irregularity of nature to a landscape more shaped and apparent, a landscape more a human construct.[6]

/ **1-2** /
GEOFFREY JELLICOE,
SHUTE HOUSE,
DORSET, ENGLAND, 1969–75.
THE CANAL GARDEN.
/ MARC TREIB /
/ **1-3** /
GEOFFREY JELLICOE,
SUTTON PLACE,
SURREY, ENGLAND, 1980–83.
THE POOL GARDEN.
WALL RELIEF BY
BEN NICHOLSON.
/ MARC TREIB /

A concern for geometry is hardly unique among landscape architects, of course, even in the twentieth century. The British landscape architect Geoffrey Jellicoe, like Le Corbusier, underscored its role in creating civilization: "The primary contribution the human mind has made to the world is its endeavor to create order from chaos. It has long been recognized that the underlying order is mathematical and this suggests that geometry is the visual expression of such order. Geometry means proportion and it is a sense of proportion that has created and stabilized the civilization of all ages."[7] In projects such as Shute House in Dorset (1969–75) and Sutton Place in Surrey (1980–83), Jellicoe fashioned the landscape as a series of rooms—rooms that stood as discrete spaces joined by movement and, at times, more formal procession [figures 1-2, 1-3]. As modernist statements Jellicoe's landscapes rarely match in purity those by Kiley. The use of the boundary hedge, the irregular grove and woodlands, and even classical statuary link Jellicoe more emphatically to a Renaissance ideal than a purely modern attitude. Although sharing affinities in geometry, *spatially* Jellicoe's landscapes rarely *flow*—unlike Kiley's landscapes which almost always do.[8] Geometry governs plan in Kiley's designs, but the spatial experience that results is all but regular.

In contrast to those landscape architects like the Danish-American Jens Jensen, who rejected orthogonal geometric order as unnatural and repugnant, to Kiley geometry was an effective vehicle for creating humane landscapes. Although at times even Jensen would employ forms with an obvious geometry—like the circle—he asserted:

> Curves represent the unchained mind full of mystery and beauty. Straight lines belong to the military thought. No mind can be free in a concept of limita-

tions. Straight lines spell autocracy, of which most European gardens are an expression, and their course points to intellectual decay, which soon develops a prison from which the mind can never escape.[9]

At times Kiley himself produced landscapes more rooted in natural patterns—especially on larger sites—but verbally he begged to differ: "When you want to copy these dumb nature scenes, I say, 'If you're going to copy, copy your ancestors—the colonial gardens.'"[10] Of course, even those designers embracing geometry may still reject its use in certain situations, like in the making of larger landscapes, for example.[11] Depending on the project Kiley could work with an order that was completely geometric, highly geometric, or a composite of geometric and naturalistic. But as a generalization, we can say that with the exception of certain grand works such as the Dulles Airport in Herndon, Virginia, or the Jefferson National Expansion Memorial in St. Louis, Kiley favored schemes rooted in a rigorous geometry: "There is an evolving, ever-changing, many-faceted order that binds everything into harmonious parts of the greater whole. Sometimes, the pervading order is violated."[12]

Kiley's early practice in architecture, and/or his life-long collaboration with architects who relied on orthogonal order, no doubt contributed to his fascination with more formal ideas of organization. Not that he always worked with straight lines and groves of trees. Masses of trees set in naturalistic swaths enclose and carefully modulate movement and views at the Jefferson National Expansion Memorial in St. Louis (Eero Saarinen, architect), for example [figure 1-4]. The landscape architect himself, however, credited the birth of his geometric awareness to his stay in Europe in the wake of World War II, while

/ 1-6 /
DAN KILEY,
LANDSCAPE ARCHITECT;
EERO SAARINEN, ARCHITECT;
NORTH CHRISTIAN CHURCH,
COLUMBUS, INDIANA, 1964.
/ MARC TREIB /

still mobilized in military service. Exposed in situ to the rigor of European cultural landscapes in general and the gardens of André Le Nôtre in particular, the young designer experienced an aesthetic awakening of sorts. "What opened my eyes and changed my approach to the act of design," he recalled late in life, "was the spatial and compositional power of these simplest of elements—this was no less than living architecture."[13] Rather than the rigid and brittle qualities that Le Nôtre's work projected in books and classes, he found a magnificence in scale and a richness in spatial play that eluded both the lens and the lecturer [figure 1-5]. From that point on—certainly by the mid-1950s—the elements of the classical landscape coalesced as his formal vocabulary. Trees—aligned, set in allées, or arranged in bosques—provide the basic elements. Sheared hedges, flower beds, pools, and fountains contribute to the prevailing order. In his landscapes these elements could be adjusted, arranged, aligned, elongated or compressed, interwoven or juxtaposed—but they remained nearly ubiquitous design elements.

Of the qualifiers listed above, perhaps the most fertile was the play between juxtaposition and interweaving—paired with the slippage that energized the regularity of the order. For the 1964 North Christian Church in Columbus, Indiana, Kiley plotted a grove of magnolia trees that embraced the church as a vegetal mantle from which the roof-as-steeple rose [figure 1-6].[14] A deft modeling of the grass-covered berms surrounded this church by Eero Saarinen, staking out the congregation's approach from the parking areas —reinforced by Kiley's walls of topiary—and guiding circulation through the building. Here the siting of the trees developed from the hexagonal geometry of the church body, generating alternate readings of the landscape as flowing outward from the nave, or inward as a green architectural

buttress. The effect is refined and calming. Yet despite this effective horizontal intertwining of architecture and landscape, little affects the space trapped vertically between the grassed ground plane and the tree canopies above it.

A similar approach propelled the design of several other projects from the 1960s. The 1963 Third Block of Independence Mall in Philadelphia used blocks of honey-locusts to erect a green barrier against the street, while creating an interplay of species and solids—and purposeful gaps in the rhythmic spacing of the trees. Water animated the voids; the rhythm, quite typically, was regular and repetitive, all enclosed by a frame of black oaks that lined the outer edges of the site.[15] A similar strategy later directed the 1978 scheme for the Dalle de La Défense in Paris, a monumental promenade extending the monumental axis originating at the Louvre [figure 1-7]. Kiley's 1962 South Garden at the Art Institute of Chicago also advanced the grid as its protagonist—here comprised of native hawthorn trees—but he adjusted the spacing of plantings along the boundary walls and positioned pools at the garden's center to avoid the potential monotony of repetition and symmetry [figure 1-8].[16] The interplay of geometry, inert materials, water, and living species was intricate and sophisticated: depressing and elevating the ground plane relieved the regularity of the gridded bosque and provided greater remove from the bustle of Michigan Avenue. The resulting spaces remain somewhat classical in tone, however, although their aberrant articulations suggest a dynamic sensibility that consciously avoided static equilibrium.

Far richer landscapes resulted when Kiley detached the tight connections between the components or interwove them as a more elaborate tapestry. Like chess pieces

/ **1-9** / *opposite above*
DAN KILEY,
LANDSCAPE ARCHITECT;
EERO SAARINEN, ARCHITECT;
MILLER GARDEN,
COLUMBUS, INDIANA, 1955.
VIEW ACROSS THE HONEY-
LOCUST ALLEE TOWARDS
THE RIVER.
/ MARC TREIB /

/ **1-10** / *opposite below*
MILLER GARDEN,
COLUMBUS, INDIANA.
THE APPLE ORCHARD
FRONTING THE STREET.
/ MARC TREIB /

/ **1-11** / *below*
MILLER GARDEN,
COLUMBUS, INDIANA.
SKYLIGHTS AT THE
INTERSECTION OF THE
WALLS AND THE EAVES
SOFTEN THE CONTRAST
BETWEEN INSIDE AND OUT;
THE TERRACE CREATES A
TRANSITION BETWEEN
HOUSE AND GARDEN.
/ MARC TREIB /

engaged in territorial combat, the blocks of bosques in these designs address one another as diverse volumes arranged in space. At times they stand side by side, independently; at other times they intermingle with their colleagues. The Miller garden explicitly reveals Kiley's spatial explorations along these lines, pitting the static swimming pool enclosure against the celebrated honey-locust allée — using this porous alignment of trees as a linear filter between the more intimate residential land-scape and the sweep of lawn that joins the house to the river below [figure 1-9]. The choice of plants reinforces Kiley's interplay of bosques and groves: the apple orchard, the redbuds, the honey-locusts, and the horse chestnuts that form the entrance allée all profit in presence from their juxtaposition. While reading first as singular units, their interweaving in space reads as an integrated whole. Seemingly paradoxically, the knitted landscapes that result are dynamic rather than stagnant. Each of the elements seems to aspire to the classical ideal of cool stasis — yet adjustments in the position and the overlapping of layers of vegetation animate the landscape's design. This lack of absolute congruence is one illustration of the slippage mentioned above.

/ REPRESENTATIVES /

There is no single date nor any one project that represents the point at which Kiley adopted slippage. And there is virtually no evidence to suggest he ever considered his practice on any theoretical, or even any conscious, level. Instead, over time, his more geometric schemes came to rely less on absolute repetition and concord, and more on an incrementally "modernized" use of the classical vocabulary. In the Miller garden, for example, slippage energized a conceptually simple layout. The plan of the

house by Eero Saarinen sets its rooms spiraling around a central living space.[17] Kiley first buffered the house from the street, using arborvitae hedges to create outdoor units that responded to the four elevations of the house. His insightful vegetal and spatial play began at the boundary hedge: at least ten-feet high, cut into roughly twenty-foot lengths, staggered in plan, and canted in section to maximize sunlight on the lower parts of the arborvitae. The stepped blocks relieved the monotony of a long single hedge — and cleverly allowed for replanting in discrete units when necessary. The outsider is tempted to look into the garden, but in fact the spacing and configuration of the hedge render peeping unfulfilled. Clipped yew blankets and flower plantings at the bases of the horse chestnuts interjected a syncopated rhythm that underscored the statement of the approach allée. Consider also the overlapping of the apple orchard with the stands of white oak [figure 1-10]. In this part of the garden Kiley exploited the high canopy of the horse chestnuts under which the intermingling trunks of the oaks and apples compose a fugal play of architectural columns. Interestingly, Kiley moored each of these move-ments with more static elements like the honey-locust allée — with its Henry Moore sculpture as terminus — and the hedged pool enclosure added at a later date. These also contributed to defining the whole: the allée operated as a colonnaded gateway between garden and the greater landscape.

To reduce the contrast in light levels between inside and out Saarinen introduced linear skylights at the intersection of the eaves and the exterior walls [figure 1-11]. This device softened the transition from interior to landscape although the plan of the house did not truly support a radical opening to the garden — at least not in the Californian sense.[18] While the heat of Indiana summers may be conducive to living outdoors for some, Midwestern winters are quite the opposite.[19] Kiley used the terraces that surround the structure in an analogous way: to provide the family with outdoor living areas, and to establish a transition between house and garden.

Slippage of a varying type informed the design of the 1965 Hamilton garden located not far from the Miller garden [figure 1-12].[20] Unlike the large acreage offered by the Miller landscape, the Hamilton site was highly constrained; yet the client asked the landscape architect to maximize the potentials for living in varied spaces. Kiley treated the garden more in the manner of a courtyard, meting the garden into distinct zones and maintaining the open lawn area as its central feature, while staking out the perimeter with contrasting intensity. To the north, a patio with swimming pool and terrace accommodated active recreation. Demonstrating another sort of slippage, Kiley overlaid an allée of honey-locusts upon the lawn with no formal trace of a path beneath them. East of the house a wall of water jets animated the garden's eastern boundary, invoking memories of Grenadine landscapes; a grove of littleleaf lindens linked house to water feature with simplicity and dignity. Expected elements appear in unexpected positions. While the basic scheme is simple, the vertical and horizontal overlay of parts energizes both movement and the definition of space. As a result, the Hamilton garden appears as classically modern or modernly classical.

This compartmentalization of garden spaces is hardly novel, although in the Hamilton garden the slippage of trees, pergola, and understory planting harvests numerous readings. Spaces rarely conclude precisely at the edge of the paving or in accord with any alignment of trunks;

/ **1-12** /
DAN KILEY,
HAMILTON GARDEN,
COLUMBUS, INDIANA, 1965.
THE LATH PAVILION WITH
ALLEE BEYOND.
/ MARC TREIB /

instead they leak into the adjacent zones and create a condition of perceptual ambiguity. In this garden—which admittedly tends to be more classical in its subdivision of the whole rather than as an agglomeration of discrete elements—the slippage is less apparent than in other Kiley projects. But one sees in its seminal form a design idea that would reach fruition in projects such as the NCNB plaza in Tampa realized two decades later. Late in life Kiley himself noted that his work had evolved, enfolding greater complexity with passing years of practice. The early projects displayed a "clarity of order-form-follows-functions" with a response to context. "By the late 1970s," he added, "designs emerging from our office were crafted landscape encounters, constructed with layers of pattern, volume and time woven together." The result, he concluded, was "the essence of infinity, the perpetration of nature's mystery."[21]

Kiley's most spectacular use of overlay and slippage directed the magnificent design of the terrace/plaza/garden for the NCNB Bank in Tampa, Florida, completed in 1988—but today sadly derelict. Here the landscape architect literally grounded his plan on the play of paved and zoysia grassed surfaces, using the numerical progressions of the Fibonacci series to determine the relative proportions of hard to soft surfaces [figures 1-13, 1-14, 1-15].[22] Moving outward from the architect Harry Wolf's cylindrical bank tower—the origin of the proportional series—the paving reversed the dominance of paved to planted surfaces. The same proportional system generated the design as an ever-changing grid that mutated constantly in all directions. A series of narrow rills—each terminating in a round basin with a single jet à la the Court of the Myrtles in the Alhambra—overlaid this carpet of numerical relations. In some areas of the garden terrace—which is, in truth,

/ 1-13 /
DAN KILEY,
LANDSCAPE ARCHITECT;
HARRY WOLF, ARCHITECT;
NCNB BANK PLAZA,
TAMPA, FLORIDA, 1988.
BENEATH THE GRID OF
PALM TREES IN THIS AREA
OF THE GARDEN, PAVING
PREDOMINATES.
/ MARC TREIB /

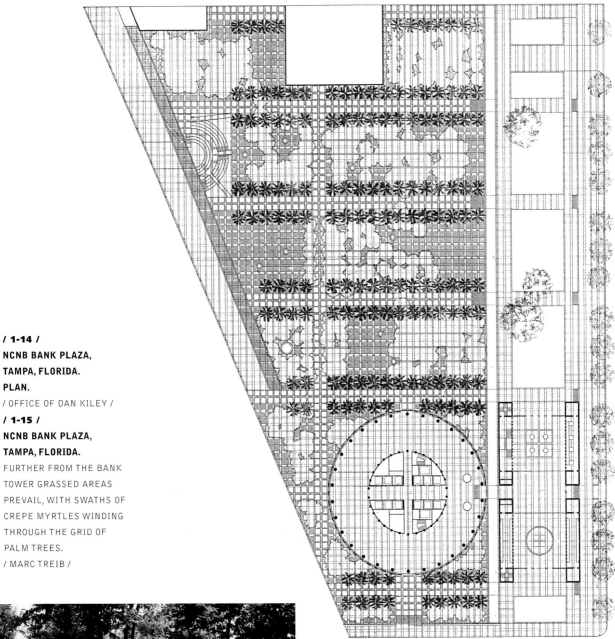

/ 1-14 /
**NCNB BANK PLAZA,
TAMPA, FLORIDA.
PLAN.**
/ OFFICE OF DAN KILEY /
/ 1-15 /
**NCNB BANK PLAZA,
TAMPA, FLORIDA.**
FURTHER FROM THE BANK
TOWER GRASSED AREAS
PREVAIL, WITH SWATHS OF
CREPE MYRTLES WINDING
THROUGH THE GRID OF
PALM TREES.
/ MARC TREIB /

a roof garden over a parking garage—shrubs further differentiated zones destined for different occupation. But on the terrace level space flowed unimpeded from the city street to the river—although at times articulated with minor stops. While a walk of major width—that essentially leads nowhere—dominated the paved areas, there is no true axis, no single direction, by which to cross the terrace. Throughout the garden the paving often suggested one direction of movement while the space and vegetation signaled others.

An orchard of sable palms constituted the scheme's dominant vertical element. As if the forecourt or hypostyle hall of an Egyptian temple translated into vegetation, their slender columns defined the project's great hall. The trunks of the palms emerged from the paving units to form the armature of the garden's composition. In counterpoint, swaths of crepe myrtles fleshed out the zones between the ground surface and the palm canopies as a contrapuntal voice to the rhythm of the palms. Planted in a seemingly "naturalistic" way, and appearing as billowing pink clouds when in flower, the clumps appeared to drift at will across paving and palms. But they too are quite precisely planted using the same gridded system. Kiley's sleight of hand demonstrates rather conclusively that an "informal" look can result from extremely "formal" plotting—it is a question of the scale of the subdivisions.[23]

Let's add up the elements of the NCNB landscape: paving based on an orthogonal system that continuously changes dimensions and proportions in both its directions; the grand stand of sentinel palms high above; and sweeps of seemingly "irregularly-spaced" crepe myrtles counter-poised against the regular geometry of the grid. This purposeful lack of congruence among the principal land-scape elements both horizontally and vertically instigates ambiguous readings that translate into experiential density apparent in section as well as in plan. Thus, while the ideas behind the planning of the terrace may smack of a classical preoccupation with numbers and proportions, the spaces resulting from that play proffer a fully modern(ist) attitude toward landscape design.

/ ARCHITECTURAL LANDSCAPES /

Dan Kiley's designs find neat parallels—but not true congruences—in the architecture of Ludwig Mies van der Rohe, the noted and at times maligned architect of steel, glass, and space. Through comparison we may identify the affinities and disparities in their work—and there are both, to be sure.

In the early 1920s Mies proposed, perhaps only as a hypothetical exercise, a country villa to be built of brick [figure 1-16]. Neither the title—Brick Country House—nor the architect provided any greater description of the purposes for the house, which was left unrealized.[24] Drawing on ideas first expounded by Frank Lloyd Wright, and later by Theo van Doesburg and others in the Dutch de Stijl group, Mies projected the spaces of the house almost as a purely architectonic composition that reached out to engage the site. In this sense, the scheme was essentially centrifugal, flowing outward from a denser internal core while reducing its defining elements to single wall planes. Rooms adjoined one another: inter-related, their definition rested to a great extent on the linear wall plane or a wall bent into the form of an L.[25] House and landscape took shape as a continuous spatial entity, with the brick wall used to bond the two. In Mies's privileging of spatial flow, one senses another sort of slippage in which space does not stop at the ostensible boundary of the house but continues, to merge with the site.

/ 1-16 /
LUDWIG MIES VAN DER ROHE,
PROJECT FOR A BRICK
COUNTRY HOUSE, 1922.
/ JAMES ROSE, "FREEDOM
IN THE GARDEN"/
/ 1-17 /
LUDWIG MIES VAN DER ROHE,
GERMAN PAVILION,
BARCELONA, SPAIN, 1929.
/ MARC TREIB /

Less than a decade later, Mies realized aspects of these ideas in the design of the German Pavilion at the Barcelona Exposition of 1929 [figure 1-17].[26] The building, which served only a ceremonial function, was primarily an investigation of architectural space, and only a single glass wall with silvery mullions differentiated the roofed interior from the unroofed courtyard beyond. The building was truly a pavilion: its two sheets of water, its rich materials, and its diminished sense of enclosure tested the limits of architectural and spatial practice at the end of the 1920s. The building provided a powerful model for both architects and landscape architects, among them Dan Kiley and his colleague Garrett Eckbo.

Compared to Mies's architectural spaces, Kiley's spaces —as landscapes—are larger, of course, and ultimately far richer—more loaded with dynamism and ambiguity, even within their essential restraint. After all, Kiley had nature on his side. Mies, for his part, in later work framed the landscape as a visual phenomenon rather than engaging with it; that is to say, the passage out to the landscape was not facilitated. [27] The register of plant species that Kiley returned to time and again was rather small; his geometry was almost always orthogonal and constrained, except in larger designs where the scale of the site precluded the use of geometry; the relation to architecture or the city was always purposeful and considerate. [28] Within a primarily architectural setting, the structuring of the building suggested a resonant response in vegetation. In Kiley's best works, however, life exists in the gaps between the landscape and the city, the landscape and the building, or between one landscape element and another: in the sites of slippage.

In the sculpture garden for the 1985 Dallas Art Museum the spaces unfold sequentially through movement, suggesting the lessons of Mies's Brick Country House project [figures 1-18, 1-19]. The fall of water and its flow along rills that glide past the bounds of the outdoor rooms enliven the essentially immobile spaces enclosed by walls. Kiley's 1985 plaza at Fountain Place, just down the street from the museum, turned virtually the entire ground plane into a crumpled sheet of falling water that spilled from one level to the next while supporting a rigorous grid of bald cypresses [figure 1-20]. The slippage here is literal rather than figurative although the layout is essentially regular. In contrast, Kiley pushed the linear pool of the 1990 Lear Garden in Los Angeles off the center of the walk and played it against a set of non-continuous retaining/ boundary walls [figure 1-21]. Coerced to some degree by topography, the composition feels like an agglomeration of parts held together by a geometric ordering always sensed but not always seen. All of these designs demonstrate that although

/ **1-18** / *opposite*
DAN KILEY,
SCULPTURE COURTYARD,
DALLAS MUSEUM OF ART,
TEXAS, 1983.
ENTRANCE WITH FOUNTAIN
WALL.
/ MARC TREIB /
/ **1-19** /
SCULPTURE COURTYARD,
DALLAS MUSEUM OF ART.
WALLS AND RILLS.
/ MARC TREIB /

/ 1-20 /
DAN KILEY,
LANDSCAPE ARCHITECT;
I. M. PEI & PARTNERS,
ARCHITECTS;
FOUNTAIN PLACE,
DALLAS, TEXAS, 1985.
/ MARC TREIB /

/ 1-21 / *opposite above*
DAN KILEY, LEAR GARDEN,
LOS ANGELES, CALIFORNIA,
1990.
/ MARC TREIB /
/ 1-22 / *opposite below*
LUDWIG MIES VAN DER ROHE,
FARNSWORTH HOUSE,
PLANO, ILLINOIS, 1951.
/ MARC TREIB /

Dan Kiley's landscapes relied on orthogonal geometry and the landscape elements of a classical tradition, they were rarely used in a classical way; nor did they result in classical gardens. Nor did they ever match in rigor and reduction such projects as Mies van der Rohe's Farnsworth house in Plano, Illinois, completed in 1951 [figure 1-22].

In a late work—the 1996 Kimmel garden in Connecticut—Kiley took on a grand site and varied his degree of control from that of the large-scale, almost regional, plan, to that of the intimate detail. Perhaps no other project evidences the landscape architect's mastery of grading and landform so well. A pool bounding the north terrace, for example, destroys the perceived edge almost as a modernist inversion of the classical ha-ha [figure 1-23]. In plan the linear basin relates to the living room of the house; in section, it addresses the hills and the skies. One senses that each of the design elements was laid down in strict accord with local demands by site, program, and house design, although a grand scheme governed the comprehensive planning of the site. No edge is sacred; vision and space boldly trespass upon each other's terrain.

/ CLASSICISM OR MODERNISM? /

A classicist? Without question, the elements—as general types—of the Kiley landscape are classical. Without question, a modernist sense of arrangement animates almost all the Kiley landscapes, a modernist/mannerist sensibility that permitted neither the bosque nor the allée to remain as a static unit unless the situation so demanded. More often, Kiley employed slippage to energize even the simplest of compositions, a slippage that permitted the intrusion of one element beyond its limits, the stacking of orders atop one another, the overlapping of one space with another—in small elements as well as large. While a geometric order is nearly ubiquitous, transgression is its constant companion. For a true understanding of the design, look not to the prevailing system of order—which is only the tool—but to its effect in generating landscape of continuing engagement and elegance.

Once, just before a client presentation, the architect Hugh Jacobsen cautioned Dan Kiley about how he should present his work: "Go easy on the geometry," he said, "because you're thought of as a neo-classicist." Kiley replied, no doubt with a characteristic impish grin, "Forget the neo."[29]

No, Dan, I really can't agree.

NOTES

An earlier version of this essay was published in *Landscape Journal*, Number 1, 2005.

1 This is an overbroad categorization, of course, and exceptions are certain to exist. In addition, even most bed planting over-grows its precise frame—but rarely to the degree of the herbaceous border in the "perennial tradition" rendered perfectly in the gardens of Gertrude Jekyll. But as an abstract idea this division of the landscape into zones is a fair, if somewhat exaggerated, characterization of classical thinking about designed landscapes.

2 Early projects such as the 1940 Charles Collier garden in Virginia used many of the design motifs then coming into fashion. "I used every cliché in the book. It had wiggles and curves and sawtooths and everything." Dan Kiley, "Lecture," in Warren T. Byrd, Jr. and Reuben M. Rainey, eds., *The Work of Dan Kiley: A Dialogue on Design Theory* (Charlottesville: University of Virginia, School of Architecture, 1982), p. 25 (reprinted in this book]). The project was left unrealized, and within a short period Kiley turned to a more restrained, more structured, approach to design. See also Dan Kiley and Jane Amidon, *Dan Kiley: The Complete Works of America's Master Landscape Architect* (Boston: Bulfinch Press, 1999), p. 12.

3 Le Corbusier, *The Modulor* (Cambridge, Mass.: Harvard University Press, 1954; reprint 1980), p. 71.

4 Kiley, "Lecture," *The Work of Dan Kiley*, p. 8.

5 Piet Mondrian, *Natural Reality and Abstract Reality: An Essay in Trialogue Form* (1919–1920), Martin S. James, trans. (New York: George Braziler, 1995), pp. 38–39.

6 In his published writings, Kiley does not mention any relationship between his own work and Mondrian's.

7 Geoffrey Jellicoe, recounting a lecture given at the Royal Academy of the Arts in 1967, in *The Guelph Lectures on Landscape Design* (Guelph: University of Guelph, 1983), p. 96.

8 A notable exception to this generalization is the biomorphically informed design of the Harvey's Roof Garden in Guildford, Surrey, designed by Jellicoe in 1951. This was, perhaps, his most modernist work—

unfortunately ruined in a recent "restoration."

9 Jens Jensen, *Siftings*, 1939 (reprint, Baltimore: Johns Hopkins University Press, 1990), p. 34. More than one author has questioned Jensen's rantings on this subject, and the political opinions behind them. Kiley took issue with naturalism and ecological fixations that denied the consequences of a particular form—as represented by Capability Brown and Ian McHarg respectively. Kiley had no problem being a contrarian, a stance that only grew in vigor as he got older. His position, while always vehement, was rarely subtly argued. "Panel Discussion," *The Work of Dan Kiley*, p. 27.

10 Kiley, "Lecture," *The Work of Dan Kiley*, p. 10. While greatly appreciative of nature and natural form—he lived in rural Vermont—Kiley rarely denied the contribution of the mind in creating landscapes for human occupation.

11 See Frank Waugh, *The Natural Style in Landscape Gardening* (Boston: Richard G. Badger, 1917).

12 Kiley and Amidon, *Dan Kiley: The Complete Works*, p. 8.

13 Ibid., p. 18.

14 Saarinen said, "On this site, with this kind of central plan, I think I would like to make the church really all one form: all tower. There would be a gradual building up of the sheltering hovering planes becoming the spire." Aline Saarinen, ed., *Eero Saarinen on His Work* (New Haven: Yale University Press, 1968), p. 98.

15 This landscape no longer exists, the victim of neglect, programmatic change, and renovation. It was demolished several years ago to make way for a transportation nexus and the National Constitution Center; Olin Partnership was the landscape architect for the new scheme. Kiley and Amidon, *Dan Kiley: The Complete Works*, pp. 42–43.

16 Ibid., pp. 48–53.

17 On the Miller garden—probably Kiley's best known work—see Gary Hilderbrand, *The Miller Garden: Icon of Modernism* (Washington, D.C.: Spacemaker Press, 1999); Gregg Bleam, "Modern and Classical Themes in the Work of Dan Kiley," in Marc Treib, ed., *Modern Landscape Architecture: A Critical Review* (Cambridge, Mass.: MIT Press, 1993), pp. 220–239; and *Process Architecture #33: Landscape Design: Works of Dan Kiley* (October 1982), pp. 20–26.

18 A typical modern Californian plan would have placed the living and dining areas adjacent to the garden to support the flow from one to the other.

19 Owning a home on the Great Lakes, the Millers may not have spent many summers in Indiana.

20 See Stacey Freed, "When Design Compels Movement," *Garden Design* (Autumn 1986), pp. 64–69.

21 Kiley, in Kiley and Amidon, *Dan Kiley: The Complete Works*, p. 92.

22 The Fibonacci series involves a mathematical progression in which each number is the sum of the two preceding numbers: 1,2,3, 5, 8, 13, etc.

23 Osmundson and Staley used a similar strategy as long ago as 1960 in the roof terrace for the Kaiser Center in Oakland, California. The major trees were positioned above the garage's columns for structural purposes; but the regularity of the planting was conclusively undermined by the biomorphic shapes of the mounds and planting beds.

24 Mies also proposed a country villa of concrete, which took considerably different form. See Wolf Tegethoff, *Mies van der Rohe: The Villas and Country Houses* (Cambridge, Mass.: MIT Press, 1985), pp. 37–51.

25 See Barry Bergdoll, "The Nature of Mies's Space," in Terence Riley and Barry Bergdoll, eds., *Mies in Berlin* (New York: Museum of Modern Art, 2001), pp. 66–105.

26 Juan Pablo Bonta, *Mies van der Rohe: The Barcelona Pavilion 1929* (Barcelona: Gustavo Gili, 1975).

27 Examples of this distancing are the 1938 project for the Resor house in Jackson Hole, Wyoming, and the celebrated all-glass 1951 Farnsworth house in Plano, Illinois.

28 There are numerous larger scale designs and campus plans—like the Dulles Airport outside Washington, D.C., and the Jefferson National Expansion Memorial in St. Louis—that do not rely on geometry to the degree we normally associate with Kiley's ideas. In a lecture he once said that he did a lot of non-geometric designs but he just tended not to show them.

29 Kiley, "Lecture," *The Work of Dan Kiley*, p. 10.

/ 2 /

Modern and Classical Themes in the Work of Dan Kiley

Gregg Bleam

Daniel Urban Kiley's 1955 design for the Miller garden played a pivotal role in his career, effectively dividing his work into two distinct periods: those projects completed between 1936 and 1954, based primarily on form as a pure art; and those created from 1955 to the present, which were derived from ideas of modern architecture. The Miller garden was Kiley's 396th project and represented a dramatic change from his previous designs. As Kiley's "first essentially modern landscape design," it expressed spatial ideas specifically adapted from Ludwig Mies van der Rohe's German Pavilion built for the 1929 World Exposition in Barcelona, Spain.[1]

The Miller house and garden were designed between 1953 and 1957 for Mr. and Mrs. J. Irwin Miller and family, on a plot of land between Washington Street and the Flatrock River in Columbus, Indiana [figure 2-1]. The house, designed by Eero Saarinen and Kevin Roche, sits on an ivy-covered marble plinth placed on a flat, square, earthen terrace approximately 15 feet above the flood plain [figure 2-2]. Kiley's design divided the site into three parts: garden, meadow, and wood [figure 2-3]. Highly ordered geometric gardens on the upper terrace surround the house and unfold as one moves through its spaces. A staggered pattern of clipped arborvitae hedges defines the boundary on three sides of this area. An allée of honey-locusts planted parallel to the west face of the house provides shade from the sun and acts as a link between a sculpture by Henry Moore to the north and a terrace and stair leading to the meadow. The meadow, originally designed to be bounded on the south by a triple row of sycamore trees, is now a mown lawn edged by a single row of red maples. Small groups of weeping willows accentuate the space. A wood adjacent to the river, consisting of flood plain trees, forms the third part of Kiley's plan. From this lower vantage point, due to the foreshortened view, the house appears to sit above a large square lawn.

/ 2-0 /
DAN KILEY,
MILLER GARDEN,
COLUMBUS, INDIANA, 1955.
THE HONEY-LOCUST ALLÉE
WITH SCULPTURE BY
HENRY MOORE.
/ MARC TREIB /

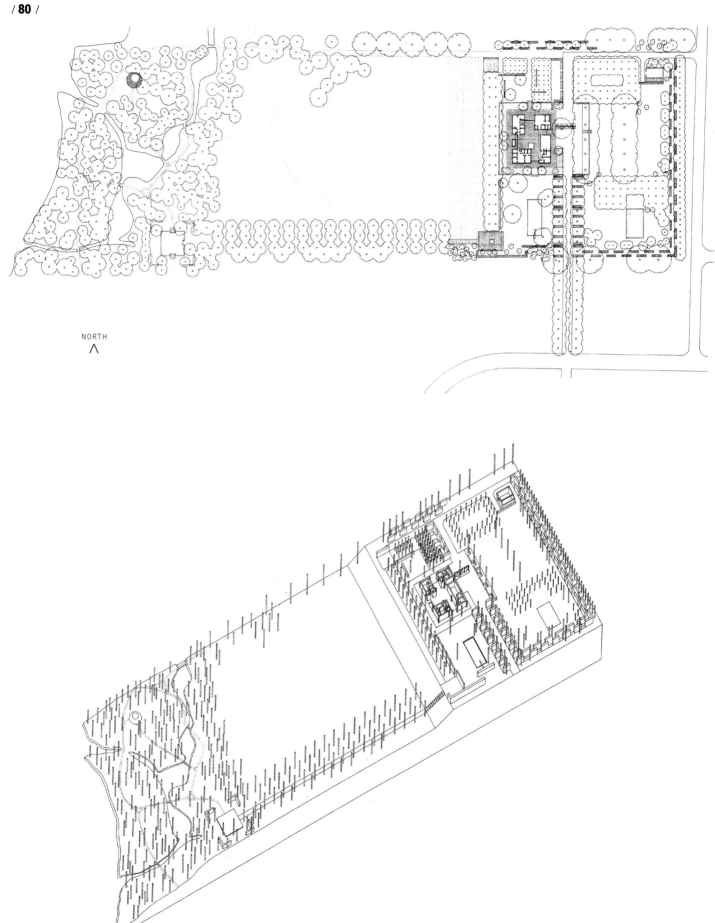

NORTH
∧

Garden, meadow, and wood create a dynamic composition reminiscent of a classical tripartite order. The spaces immediately surrounding the house, however, are not classically structured; they are based upon a much different—and modern—spatial sensibility.

A comparison of the Miller garden with Kiley's previous designs raises questions concerning the reasons for the radical shift in his design vocabulary in the mid-1950s. To answer these questions, it is necessary first to establish the figures and events that were shaping his career.

/ BACKGROUND: KILEY'S EARLY WORK /

Kiley was born in Boston, Massachusetts, in 1912 and worked in the office of landscape architect Warren Manning from 1932 to 1938. In February 1936 he enrolled as a special student in the landscape architecture program at Harvard University, against the advice of Manning. There he encountered Garrett Eckbo and James Rose, who joined him in rejecting the prevalent Beaux-Arts education in order to explore themes related to modern art and architecture. In particular, the three students were influenced by the work of Walter Gropius, who was teaching at Harvard at that time. One year later, Kiley left Harvard without a diploma and moved to Washington, D.C. He began working for the United States Housing Authority as the Associate Town Planning Architect, a job previously held by Eckbo. Elbert Peets, the well-known landscape architect and town planner, was his supervisor. While working at the agency he met Louis Kahn, who offered him the opportunity to work on several Defense War Housing projects. Kiley quickly accepted, and Kahn became the first of many architects with whom he would collaborate

throughout his prolific career. Kahn also introduced Kiley to a young architect named Eero Saarinen, perhaps one of his most important introductions.[2]

Kiley left the Housing Authority in 1940 and opened the Office of Dan Kiley in Washington, D.C., and Franconia, New Hampshire. His first commission was a garden for the 40-acre Collier residence, in Falls Church, Virginia, in Kiley's words "a 'modernistic' house, but not modern" [figures 2-4 and 2-5].[3] The forms he used in the garden's plan were curvilinear and featured an undulating copse, juxtaposed with clipped hedges arranged in a chevron pattern; a secret garden; a vegetable garden; a children's play area; and a curving line of flowering yoshino cherries surrounding a central lawn, divided by an existing row of eastern red cedars. For four months during the garden's realization, the landscape architect lived with the Colliers, personally completing the site grading and supervising the extensive plantings.

In 1940, Kiley also designed numerous small residential projects including the Kenneth Kassler garden in Princeton, New Jersey, and the A. A. S. Davy garden in Middleburg, Virginia. The Kassler and Davy designs were published in 1941 by Garrett Eckbo in *The Magazine of Art*, as examples of "fresh use of indigenous traditional material." In this article Eckbo aptly described the themes that he and Kiley were exploring at this time, which stemmed from ideas about the rural landscape:

> *And there we do find innumerable definite three-dimensional space forms produced with both structural and natural material: rectangular or polygonal fields cut from solid natural wildwoods: trees in rows or belts*

/ **2-1** / *opposite above*
MILLER GARDEN,
COLUMBUS, INDIANA, 1955.
PLAN.

/ **2-2** / *opposite below*
MILLER GARDEN,
AXONOMETRIC DIAGRAM.

/ **2-3** / *right*
MILLER GARDEN,
ZONING DIAGRAM.

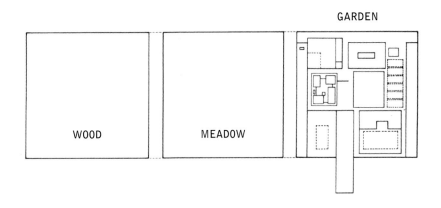

GARDEN

WOOD   MEADOW

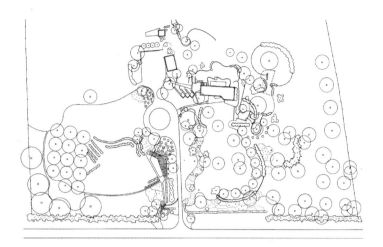

*forming planes: the regularity of orchards: straight
lines of untrimmed hedges and mixed hedgerows,
and of fences and old stone walls, grown up with
natural plants: free-standing clumps of trees forming
natural pavilions: intersecting planes of these lines of
trees and hedges and walls forming a fragmentary
organization of space.*[4]

In a similar vein, Kiley completed a garden for the planner
Edmund Bacon in 1941 and collaborated on several large
housing projects with Louis Kahn, including the Lily Pond
Housing Project in Washington, D.C., of 1942. Many of
these designs strongly recalled the biomorphic forms
associated with the work of Eckbo and Rose; there was
not yet evidence of the geometric purity and classical
references now typically associated with Kiley's designs.

During the war years—between 1942 and 1944—Kiley
served in the Army Corps of Engineers. In 1944 he replaced
Eero Saarinen in the Office of Strategic Services, in Fort
Belvoir, Virginia, at the latter's request. Also in 1944 Kiley
collaborated on his first project with Saarinen, moon-
lighting on a design competition for a new Parliament
Building in Quito, Ecuador. In 1945 Saarinen returned to
Michigan to assist his father Eliel on the design of the
General Motors Technical Center in Warren, Michigan.
Eero invited Kiley to collaborate on this project, but Kiley,
still in active service, could not accept the invitation. Instead,
he recommended three colleagues: Thomas Church, Garrett
Eckbo, and James Rose.[5] Saarinen selected Church for
the project that would become Saarinen's most complete
architectural expression of modernism embracing a neoclassical landscape.[6]

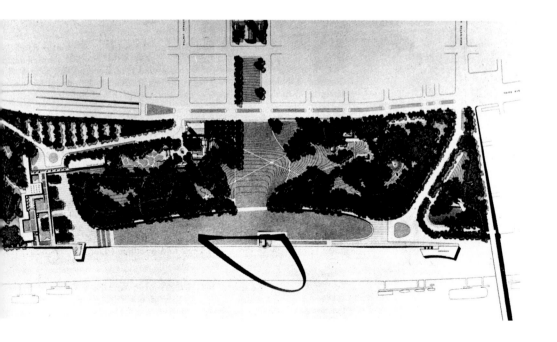

/ 2-4 /
COLLIER RESIDENCE,
FALLS CHURCH, VIRGINIA,
1940. PLAN.

/ 2-5 /
COLLIER RESIDENCE,
FIGURE-GROUND DIAGRAM.

/ 2-6 /
DAN KILEY,
LANDSCAPE ARCHITECT;
EERO SAARINEN,
ARCHITECT;
JEFFERSON NATIONAL
EXPANSION MEMORIAL,
ST. LOUIS, MISSOURI, 1947.
PLAN.
/ OFFICE OF DAN KILEY /

Upon Saarinen's departure from the Office of Strategic Services, Kiley assumed his position as Chief of the Design Presentation Branch and was named as the architect for the Nuremburg Trials Courtroom in Germany.[7] This assignment afforded him the opportunity to visit Europe for the first time. While overseas, he saw the great gardens of Versailles and Parc du Sceaux, classic seventeenth-century designs by André Le Nôtre. This exposure to Le Nôtre's work—its simplicity, clarity of geometric order, and restraint—proved important in Kiley's development and would become the basis for his synthesis of a classical vocabulary with ideas of modern space in the landscape.

Following the war, Kiley moved his office to Franconia, New Hampshire, mainly because, in his words, it offered "good skiing." Practicing primarily as an architect, in 1946 he completed several small houses, including a "modernized New England farmhouse" for B. M. Kimball in New Hampshire and a flat-roofed modern house for John Atherton in Arlington, Vermont.[8] Both projects transformed the materials found in vernacular houses of the rural northeast into a modernist vocabulary.

In 1947, he collaborated again with Eero Saarinen on an entry for the Jefferson Expansion Memorial Competition in St. Louis, Missouri, which they won [figure 2-6]. Both architect and landscape architect benefited from the widespread attention focused on their collaborative effort, even though completion of the project was stalled until the early 1960s.[9] Kiley completed other projects on his own at this time, including a landscape plan for the David Hamilton garden, in Princeton, New Jersey, in 1949— which featured an entrance court planting of thyme planted in a grid pattern.[10] In 1951 he moved his residence and

office to a site on Lake Champlain, facing the Adirondack Mountains, in Charlotte, Vermont. That same year he designed a series of gardens for Minoru Yamasaki's Louis Baker house in Greenwich, Connecticut, that spiraled from the center of the house outward into the wooded site [figure 2-7].[11] Just prior to the Miller garden, in 1954, Saarinen recommended Kiley as landscape architect for the Robert Osborn residence, in Salisbury, Connecticut. Edward Larrabee Barnes was the architect of this Mies-inspired, bilaterally symmetrical house, published in Barnes's 1956 article "Platform Houses."[12] Here, Kiley proposed his most geometric planting design to date, consisting of an entrance drive allée of elms and a bosque of red maples planted on a grid [figure 2-8]. A gravel parking court, surrounded by hedges planted parallel and perpendicular to the house, sequenced the arrival. To the south of the house lay an herb garden planted in a checker-board pattern, similar to that proposed for the David Hamilton garden. In the Osborn plan, there is a clear movement away from the fragmented forms of Kiley's earlier designs in favor of a new, geometric order (compare the figure-ground diagrams in figures 2-5 and 2-9).

In 1955, Kiley began work with Eero Saarinen on the Miller garden. Working with the established order of Saarinen's house afforded Kiley the opportunity to explore more completely the potentials of Neoplatonic geometric forms. The architect allowed Kiley the freedom to integrate the house with the surrounding garden using a shared geometric order. A comparison of Saarinen's landscape ideas with those of Mies van der Rohe will illuminate the differences in the two architects' approaches and further articulate the formal concepts that Saarinen brought to the Miller design.

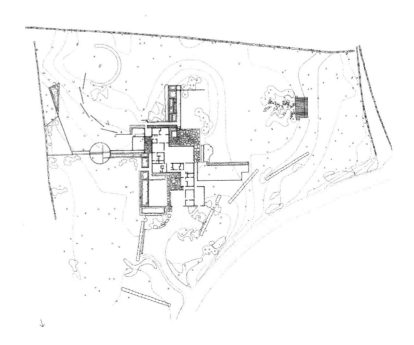

/ 2-7 /
DAN KILEY,
LANDSCAPE ARCHITECT;
MINORU YAMASAKI,
ARCHITECT;
BAKER HOUSE,
GREENWICH, CONNECTICUT,
1951. SITE PLAN.

/ EERO SAARINEN AND MIES VAN DER ROHE /

Unlike many architects of his time, Saarinen placed a high value on the integration of architecture with outdoor space. In a lecture at Dickinson College in 1959, he expressed this commitment:

> I see architecture not as building alone, but the building in relation to its surroundings, whether nature or man-made surroundings. I believe that the single building must be carefully related to the whole in the outdoor space it creates. In its mass and scale and material it must become an enhancing element in the total environment. Now this does not mean that the building has to succumb to the total. Any architecture must hold its head high. But a way must be found for uniting the whole, because the total environment is more important than the single building.[13]

This position was not generally held by many architects practicing during the 1940s and 50s, who typically used plants only as a foil for their buildings rather than as structural elements to connect interior and exterior space. Saarinen, trained in the Beaux-Arts method at Yale University, carried forth both his father Eliel Saarinen's philosophy and the Scandinavian tradition of creating an architecture that benefited from a reciprocal relationship with the landscape.[14]

Throughout the years that constitute Eero Saarinen's early career, the architecture of Mies van der Rohe transformed the practice of architecture. Numerous young architects, including Saarinen himself, followed Mies's lead in adopting a strain of functionalism that utilized neoclassical design principles. "The preference for simple geometrical forms ... and the assembly of a number of disparate volumes" was tempered initially by asymmetry—which eventually

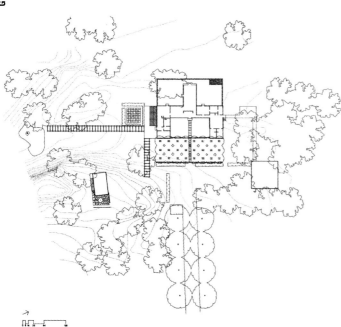

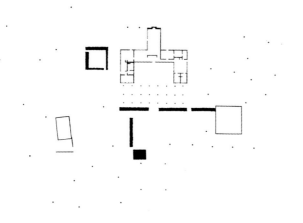

/ 2-8 /
DAN KILEY,
LANDSCAPE ARCHITECT;
EDWARD LARRABEE
BARNES, ARCHITECT;
OSBORN RESIDENCE,
SALISBURY, CONNECTICUT,
1954. PLAN.

/ 2-9 /
OSBORN RESIDENCE,
FIGURE-GROUND DIAGRAM.

became almost complete symmetry.[15] Saarinen's General Motors Technical Center is a clear example of this formal transformation, whose prototype was provided by Mies's master plan (begun 1939) for the Illinois Institute of Technology in Chicago, Illinois [figures 2-10 to 2-15]. Concurrent with the GM Technical Center project, Saarinen was engaged in numerous campus master plans across the country, such as Antioch College in Yellow Springs, Ohio, and Drake University in Des Moines, Iowa. His was perhaps the best known campus design firm in the country; their knowledge of campus master planning allowed for a logical point of departure for the design of the GM headquarters.[16] Without the need for incorporating existing buildings into the plan, Saarinen and Thomas Church could establish the character of landscape and buildings throughout.

A comparison of Saarinen's GM Technical Center with Mies's master plan for the Illinois Institute of Technology reveals two very different attitudes about a building's relationship to the landscape. At IIT a "picturesque" landscape designed by the Prairie School landscape architect Alfred Caldwell (a disciple of Jens Jensen) surrounds Mies's classically proportioned buildings, almost like a Greek temple on a natural site. Caldwell's IIT planting plan denied any orthogonal relationship with the buildings that might have extended the organization of the buildings into the surrounding outdoor spaces [figure 2-15]. Conversely, the Saarinen and Church plan at GM created a highly ordered, classical landscape that effectively extended the geometry of the buildings directly into the landscape [see figure 2-12]. In 1956, *Architectural Forum* titled the campus project "GM's Industrial Versailles," clearly alluding to the design's vast scale and the underlying classical order of the plan.[17] Trees were planted in straight lines derived from the buildings' geometry, and hedges were clipped to define surrounding outdoor spaces. This commitment to a highly ordered landscape continued throughout Saarinen's career.

Saarinen's projects immediately following the General Motors campus remained within the Miesian idiom with respect to the architecture. Most notable is the Irwin Union Bank and Trust Company of 1952 to 1955 in Columbus, Indiana, where he used a nine-square grid of columns to create a classically inspired bank. Unlike Mies, however, Saarinen was steadfast in his belief in a highly ordered, geometric landscape. Collaborating with Dan Kiley on most of his major commissions was a natural outcome of this belief; the importance that Saarinen assigned to the landscape, furthermore, was crucial in creating the Miller garden.

/ THE BARCELONA PAVILION AND THE MILLER HOUSE /

Mies's Barcelona Pavilion is now considered one of the key structures of modern architecture [figure 2-16]. Although the pavilion stood but six months (until its recent reconstruction), it was included in both *The International Style* of 1932, by Henry-Russell Hitchcock and Philip Johnson —which accompanied an exhibition at the Museum of Modern Art—and *Gardens in the Modern Landscape*, Christopher Tunnard's polemic of 1938. Kiley first studied the pavilion in architectural periodicals as a student at Harvard University. Through these publications, Kiley, Garrett Eckbo, and scores of other designers became familiar with this seminal work.[18]

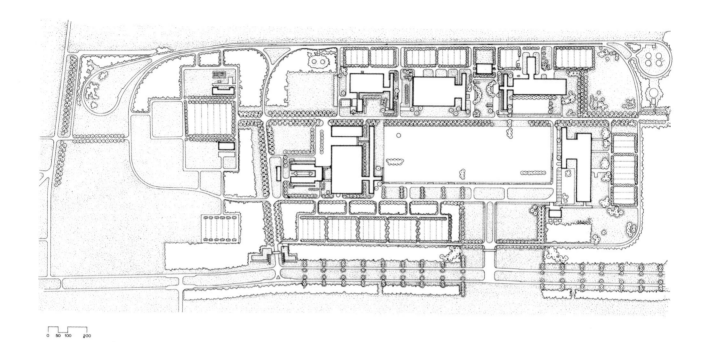

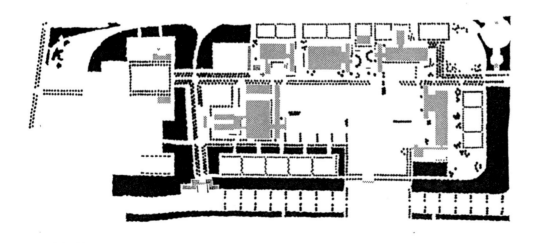

/ 2-10 /
EERO SAARINEN, ARCHITECT;
THOMAS CHURCH,
LANDSCAPE ARCHITECT;
GENERAL MOTORS
TECHNICAL CENTER,
WARREN, MICHIGAN, 1953.
SITE PLAN,

/ 2-11 /
GENERAL MOTORS
TECHNICAL CENTER,
WARREN, MICHIGAN.
FIGURE-GROUND DIAGRAM.

/ 2-12 /
GENERAL MOTORS
TECHNICAL CENTER,
WARREN, MICHIGAN.
FIGURE-GROUND
PLANTING DIAGRAM.

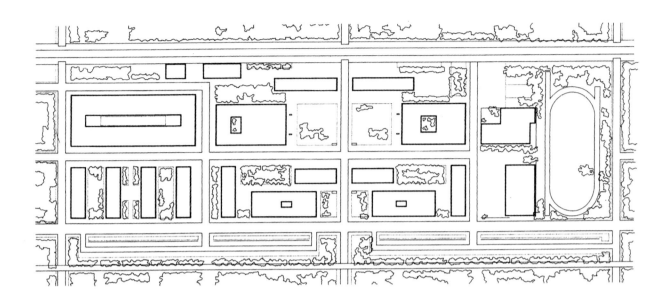

/ 2-13 /
LUDWIG MIES VAN DER ROHE,
ARCHITECT;
ALFRED CALDWELL,
LANDSCAPE ARCHITECT;
ILLINOIS INSTITUTE
OF TECHNOLOGY, CHICAGO,
ILLINOIS, 1939–1940.
SITE PLAN.

/ 2-14 /
ILLINOIS INSTITUTE
OF TECHNOLOGY,
CHICAGO, ILLINOIS.
FIGURE-GROUND DIAGRAM.

/ 2-15 /
ILLINOIS INSTITUTE
OF TECHNOLOGY,
CHICAGO, ILLINOIS.
FIGURE-GROUND
PLANTING DIAGRAM.

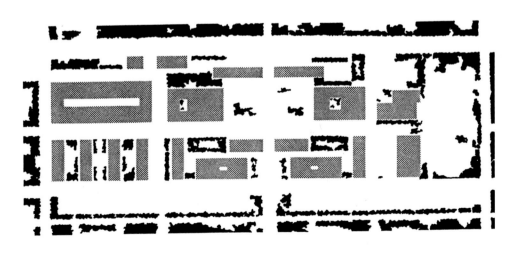

Kiley later said, "The Barcelona Pavilion said it all, the way the walls went... We were fascinated with that and the spatial idea."[19] The structural system of the pavilion consisted of a grid of eight cruciform columns set upon a podium; its spaces were modulated by freestanding walls that appeared to slide through space. This juxtaposition of vertical column with horizontal plane allows the pavilion to be spatially ambiguous, with a single center always denied and space flowing continuously. "It represents two important developments in Mies's work: the 'free plan' and the concept of a spatial continuum," writes David Spaeth:

> In the free plan, walls are liberated from their load bearing function, becoming light screens or planes in space...The other idea that Mies articulated in the Barcelona Pavilion is that space exists as a continuum. It has the characteristic of a Möbius strip in that as one moved through the pavilion, what was once perceived as inside was in actuality outside. Floor, roof, and wall planes do not contain the space but define it, clarifying and articulating its existence. As a result, the pavilion exhibits profound structural clarity; simultaneously, it is spatially ambiguous.[20]

This spatial idea, previously explored by Mies in his Brick Country House design of 1922, unified Frank Lloyd Wright's concepts of free-flowing space and de Stijl painter Theo van Doesburg's use of overlapping geometric planes.

De Stijl spatial concepts also affected Garrett Eckbo, who was fascinated with the Barcelona Pavilion as a Harvard graduate student and a fledgling practitioner. In his thesis project for a "Hypothetical Superblock Park," he boldly featured the Barcelona Pavilion as a community center.[21] Eckbo's exploration of these Miesian ideas culminated in his 1940 design for a garden in Menlo Park, California,

in which an existing orchard of pear trees was transformed by a series of hedges arranged in a pinwheel configuration [figure 2-17]. The influence of Mies on the Menlo Park design was acknowledged by Eckbo in his book *Landscape for Living*: "Living and dining spaces relate easily and naturally to a large rear garden, organized with straight rough hedges and structural extensions from the house into a kind of free rectangularity, reminiscent of de Stijl-van der Rohe planning."[22]

While Eckbo had explored Miesian space at the beginning of his career, Dan Kiley did not show similar interests until almost fifteen years later in his design for the Miller garden. By this time Kiley was 43 years old and a seasoned practitioner. Several fortuitous circumstances—the Miller garden client, the relatively flat open site of approximately ten acres, and the precedent of Saarinen's Miesian house—created the ideal climate for Kiley to translate Mies van der Rohe's spatial concepts into the garden.

The architects Eero Saarinen and Kevin Roche and interior architect Alexander Girard had designed the Miller house during a period in the early 1950s when other architects (including Louis Kahn, John Johansen, Philip Johnson, and Mies van der Rohe) were moving away from the asymmetrical forms of modern architecture to more symmetrical buildings. These buildings were termed "neo-Palladian" by the architectural critic Colin Rowe: "Most generally the contemporary neo-'Palladian' building presents itself as a small house equipped with Miesian elevation and details. Conceptually a pavilion and usually a single volume, it aspires to a rigorous symmetry of exterior and (where possible) interior."[23]

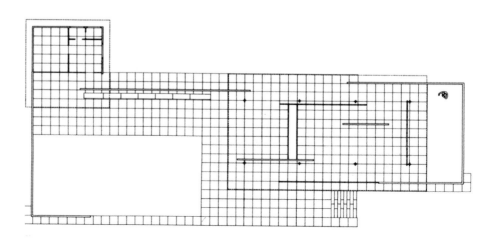

/ 2-16 /
LUDWIG MIES VAN DER ROHE,
GERMAN PAVILION,
BARCELONA, SPAIN, 1929.
GRID PLAN.

Architectural Forum published the Miller house in 1958 and referred to it as "a contemporary Palladian villa," comparing the Miller plan with a diagram of Andrea Palladio's Villa Rotonda.[24] This comparison requires some imagination. In contrast to the Villa Rotonda's strongly centered plan, the theoretical center of the Miller house (the "conversation pit") is shifted off center and is not clearly defined due to the pinwheel configuration of rooms and doors [figure 2-18].

The Miller house is supported by 16 white cruciform columns arranged to form a nine-square grid. These structural columns support the steel frame, articulating the distinction between column, wall, and horizontal roof, a characteristic of Mies's mature architecture. Organized on a grid module of 2'-6", the free interior plan allows the four individual "houses" (or rooms) to accommodate the different programmatic needs of parents, children, guests, and service. Spatially, each of these rooms pinwheels around the ambiguous center of the house, providing Kiley with a model with which to design the surrounding garden.

/ THE MILLER GARDEN AS MODERNIST FORM /

Kiley's study of 1955 [figure 2-19] differs programmatically (but not diagrammatically) from the most frequently published garden plan of 1957 [see figure 2-1]. In an early drawing of this unbuilt design, a horse paddock was proposed in the meadow and a stable under the sloping grass bank northwest of the house. Vegetable gardens and a tennis court also appear in this early scheme, but both were eliminated when the Millers decided to move them to an adjacent lot.[25] The zoning of the garden, relating to the interior functions of the house, is apparent in this early plan. Kiley placed the parents' room next to the adult garden, private garden, and dining panel. Service functions were located adjacent to the kitchen garden, laundry yard, greenhouse, vegetable gardens, and orchards. Guests were housed near tennis, swimming, and the arrival lawn. Children also had a defined lawn area for play, as well as access to the recreational areas of the garden. These program elements were organized as a series of overlapping spaces that, due to the placement of the driveway and honey-locust allée, suggested a centrifugal movement similar to the plan of the house.[26] Except for those changes mentioned above, the essence of this diagram [figure 2-20] did not change in the published design of 1957.

Additional sources for Kiley's design at the Miller garden were numerous. One must acknowledge the more intuitive aspects of design formed by Kiley's relationship to the client and by the project's site conditions. Also, Kiley's admiration for the classical geometries of Le Nôtre's gardens is evident in his design vocabulary for the Miller garden. In the plan of 1955, for example, vegetable gardens are organized along the lines of a French potager; and a dense allée of horse chestnut trees—a common Le Nôtre device—leads to the entrance court of the house. Bosques, clipped hedges, tapis vert, and crushed-stone walks also recall the gardens of Le Nôtre. Kiley dismissed complicated explanations: "The house was designed in functional blocks, such as the kitchen, the dining room, the master bedroom, and the living room. So I took this same geometry and made rooms outside using trees in groves and allées."[27]

Nevertheless, the influence of the Barcelona Pavilion as a model of modern spatial ideas can readily be seen in

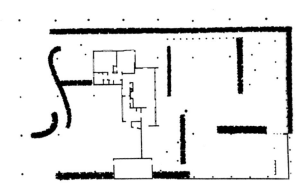

/ **2-17** /
GARRETT ECKBO,
GARDEN IN MENLO PARK,
CALIFORNIA, 1940.
FIGURE-GROUND DIAGRAM.

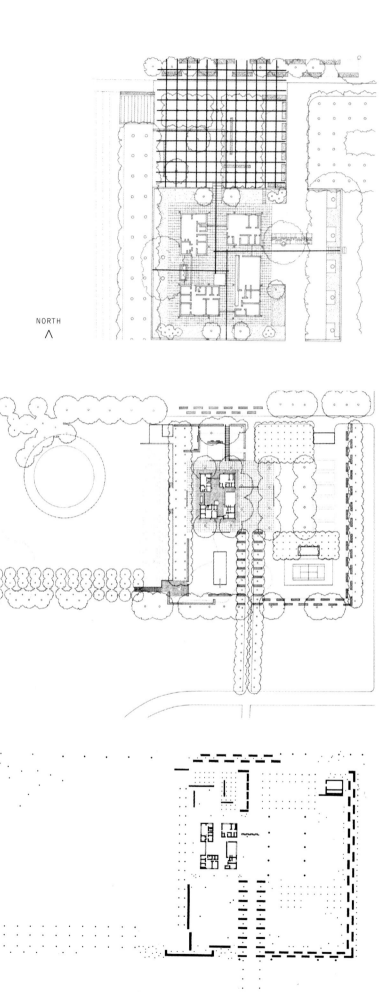

NORTH
∧

the Miller garden. Indeed, a more comprehensive comparison of the two schemes reveals that the Barcelona Pavilion and, specifically, the adult section of the Miller garden [figure 2-21] share five design characteristics: neoclassicism, the grid, asymmetry, horizontality, and de Stijl space.

/ NEOCLASSICISM /

Philip Johnson wrote in 1947 that Mies's pavilion contained "in the elevation of the structure on a podium, a touch of Schinkel," alluding to German architect Karl Friedrich Schinkel, whose neoclassical designs influenced Mies.[28] Kenneth Frampton has also noted the pavilion's indebtedness to the classical language: "The eight columns regularly spaced on a square grid and symmetrical with regard to the flat slab they support may be read as a metaphor for a classical belvedere."[29] This podium alludes to Schinkel's highly romantic design for the Hofgärtnerei in the park in Potsdam; as an element of classical architecture the podium also contrasts with the modern spatial configuration Mies created through the use of walls as freestanding planes.

Elsewhere, architects of the 1950s were being reintroduced to the neoclassical roots of modern architecture. Rudolf Wittkower's *Architectural Principles in the Age of Humanism* promoted a return to plans based upon Neoplatonic and neoclassical ideals.[30] This attitude was similarly described by Reyner Banham in his *Theory and Design in the First Machine Age* of 1960, which presented functionalism as a reinterpretation of neoclassical principles (in which the forerunners of modernism had been trained). Banham elaborated his position in the entry for "Neo-classicism" in the *Encyclopedia of Modern Architecture*, and noted the ambiguity in calling a project "classical" and at the same time "modern."[31] Perhaps more than any other architect of his time, Mies represented a synthesis of what would seem to be the conflicting conceptions of neoclassicism and modernism.[32]

Dan Kiley's Miller garden also represented a synthesis of modern spatial ideas and classical structure. Speaking of this fusion Kiley has said: "I find direct and simple expressions of function and site to be the most potent. In many cases, though not all, this has led me to design using classic geometries to order spaces that are related in a continuous spatial system that indicates connections beyond itself, ultimately with the universe."[33] The Miller garden's classical garden elements of allée, bosque, clipped hedge, and tapis vert are juxtaposed with modern spatial concepts. Bosques of redbud trees planted on a grid form an L-shaped space that defines two sides of the tapis vert. The ingenious placement of the honey-locust allée leading to the Henry Moore sculpture (added in the 1960s) runs counter to the tripartite movement of garden to meadow to wood; as a transparent wall on the western edge of the garden, it creates what Kiley has referred to as a "balustrade" in front of the platform of the house.[34] Kiley's synthesis might be seen as a response to Joseph Hudnut's admonition of 1948:

> We must continue our search for some basis of formalization if we are to create a garden for the modern house. Perhaps we can discover this basis within the house: some principle of order which, extended beyond its wall, is destined to overcome the order, or disorder, of its surroundings. One such

/ **2-18** / *opposite above*
DAN KILEY,
LANDSCAPE ARCHITECT;
EERO SAARINEN, ARCHITECT;
MILLER HOUSE AND GARDEN,
COLUMBUS, INDIANA, 1955.
FLOOR PLAN / AXES
DIAGRAM.

/ **2-19** / *opposite center*
MILLER GARDEN.
STUDY PLAN, 1955.

/ **2-20** / *opposite below*
MILLER GARDEN.
FIGURE-GROUND DIAGRAM.

/ **2-21** / *right*
MILLER GARDEN,
ADULT GARDEN.
AXONOMETRIC DRAWING.

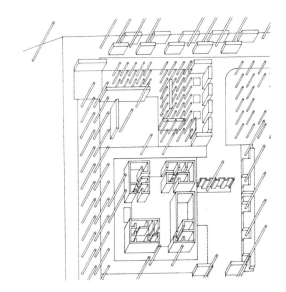

principle at least has been suggested: that very provocative principle which is called functionalism.[35] Functionalism provided Kiley, and other Miesian-influenced architects practicing at the time, with the opportunity to begin with a classical parti and then transform it by using asymmetrically placed walls and spaces, all ultimately controlled by the pure geometry of the square.

/ THE GRID /

The grid is certainly not an idea unique to our times, for it dates as far back as the Egyptian garden where date palms were planted in regular patterns. Early in the twentieth century, however, the grid became a symbol of all that was modern in art and architecture. Rosalind Krauss has written: "By 'discovering' the grid, cubism, de Stijl, Mondrian, Malevich... landed in a place that was out of reach of everything that went before, which is to say they landed in the present and everything else was declared to be the past."[36] Architecture's focus on developing forms that decentralized space and emphasized the periphery also took advantage of the continuous order the grid allowed. The grid was ideal for extending the boundaries of the building in all directions; through its repetition, it abolished the center and moved the viewer's eyes to the periphery, implying a continuous, nonhierarchical order. Le Corbusier's Maison Domino of 1914 illustrates the importance of the column grid as a support for the concrete floors above, making the free plan possible. There are also numerous instances of the adaptation of the grid in the formation of the twentieth-century garden. Walter Gropius's own house of 1938 in Lincoln, Massachusetts, was placed in the midst of a skewed grid of an existing apple orchard; Garrett Eckbo

utilized the grid of an existing pear orchard, as mentioned previously, to organize his garden at Menlo Park.

In the Miller project, both Saarinen's house and Kiley's garden relied on the grid as a basic organizational device. Besides its modernist credentials, the grid had a regional appropriateness as well; for no form is more emblematic of the American Midwest as the module for farm, town, and city on the plains. Saarinen regulated the placement of walls and columns with a 2'-6"-square grid module that extends from the interior to the exterior podium of the house. Kiley also used a 10-foot grid to regulate the location of trees and hedges, although the podium grid of the house and the regulating grid of the garden are not aligned in plan. Other grids were used throughout the garden, in many instances inconsistent with one another, emphasizing the independence of rooms within the garden. In plan, these grids create a pattern that reinforces the centrifugal movement of space around the house. By defining a structure (the column of trees) that could be countered with walls (hedges), Kiley approximated the architectural concept of the free plan.

/ ASYMMETRY /

Asymmetry, another characteristic of the Miller design, was also a hallmark of modernism. Walter Gropius, who taught in the architecture program at Harvard University during Kiley's enrollment, wrote in 1923 of the "new" principle of asymmetrical composition: "At the same time the symmetrical relationship of parts of a building and their orientation towards a central axis is being replaced by a new conception of equilibrium which transmutes this dead symmetry of similar parts into an asymmetrical but rhythmical balance."[37] This denial of the axis and

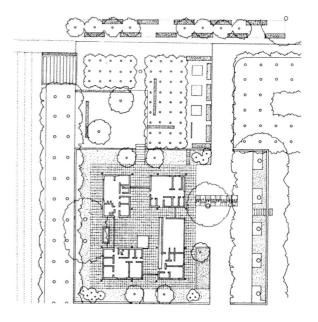

/ 2-22 /
MILLER GARDEN,
ADULT GARDEN.
PLANTING DIAGRAM.

preference for asymmetrical composition was fully expressed in Mies's pavilion at Barcelona. The asymmetrical organization of the plan counters the classical form of the podium and supports the free-plan organization of walls. The nonaxial entry to the pavilion and the nonalignment of the main pool with the pavilion proper also serve to heighten the contrast between classical and modern traditions [see figure 2-16].

The Miller garden also presents a series of asymmetrical overlapping forms. This composition draws not only on modernism but also on Japanese design. Christopher Tunnard's *Gardens in the Modern Landscape* identified asymmetry as a hallmark of the modern garden and cited the example of the Japanese house. Similarly Kiley stated: "It is the Japanese house which excites me and influences my design with its ordering of continuous, interpenetrating spaces into a serviceable and unified whole."[38] Asymmetries abound in the adult portion of the Miller garden, beginning with the nonalignment of the lawn panels [figure 2-22]. Upon this "square" of lawn, two specimen yellowwood trees are asymmetrically placed. One enters this portion of the garden from the house alongside a rectangular bosque of redbud trees, which leads to a small fountain on axis with the house door but off center with the space. These trees bound the northern and eastern sides of the garden room, while the honey-locust allée borders the western edge of the space.

/ HORIZONTALITY /

At the Bauhaus, Gropius had promoted the "new aesthetic of the horizontal" that stemmed from the publication of Frank Lloyd Wright's work in the Wasmuth portfolio of 1910 and 1911. The Wrightian emphasis on the horizontal exerted a great influence on the work of Mies van der Rohe; it is evident in the disposition of the Barcelona Pavilion's cantilevered horizontal roof planes and their extension beyond the walls. Through these devices, the relationship of building to landscape is reinforced as the planar roof appears to hover over the ground plane.

Horizontality also dominates the Miller house and garden. Saarinen's house, a one-story rectangle in plan, has a roof that cantilevers over the surrounding podium, helping to define a transitional space between house and garden. Kiley reinforces this horizontality by evergreen plantings of arborvitae hedges clipped to a uniform height of 12 feet that function as long walls, in turn defining the edges of the garden. Geometric grid plantings of trees of the same species and height, such as the redbud bosques and honey-locust allée, reinforce the horizontal dimension of the adult garden. Set against the flat floor of lawn and crushed stone, these horizontally branching plants reinforce the planar quality of the garden. The emphasis on the horizontal is especially clear when the house is viewed from the flood plain woods below. From this position, house and garden merge; the white house is set like a jewel in a green box, screened by the long horizontal line of the allée. The sharp incline creates a plinth for the house and garden and highlights the ever-present horizon line, so clearly expressed by Mies and Wright.

/ DE STIJL SPACE /

The Barcelona Pavilion's design creates a horizontal, centrifugal space through the arrangement of freestanding planes and cruciform columns. While undeniably Wrightian in origin (one need only compare the plans of Wright's Gerts House of 1906 and Mies's Brick Country House of 1922), it is a transformation of Wright's theories into the spatial concepts of de Stijl.[39] Although Mies denied the influence of de Stijl on his work, there is a strong visual connection in his buildings prior to 1930 with the paintings of Theo van Doesburg, founder of the de Stijl movement. This connection has most often been made through a comparison of van Doesburg's painting *Rhythm of a Russian Dance* of 1918 with Mies's plan for the Brick Country House. James Rose illustrated this comparison in his 1938 article "Freedom in the Garden," calling it an example of the "recognizable continuity of the contemporary style, from pattern to architecture to landscape."[40]

The abstract paintings of Piet Mondrian, which presented portions of an ordered system that was hypothetically infinite, are perhaps the clearest expression of the de Stijl aesthetic. These paintings were based upon a theosophic, cosmic vision of space derived from the philosopher Schoenmaekers and ultimately based on platonic ideas.[41] So, too, Kiley (although certainly not a theosophist) speaks of the spiritual and of a "cosmic awareness" whereby he attempts "to express this connectedness with the universe" in his design approach.[42]

This notion of de Stijl space can be seen in the Miller garden in the form created by the small Japanese holly hedges originally planted in the adult garden [figure 2-23]. Kiley's hedges were placed between the square grid of redbud tree trunks in a manner similar (at least in plan) to the walls and columns of the Barcelona Pavilion. This arrangement parallels Eckbo's use of hedges around the lawn at Menlo Park, but Kiley chose to use the same evergreen plant for all of the hedges, whereas Eckbo used a different plant for each hedge (in some instances flowering), thereby weakening the purity of the space. Unfortunately, with the removal of Kiley's "pinwheel" hedges from the adult garden, the ideas of spatial continuum and free-plan space were lost in this portion of the garden. Kiley has stated that "the major thing that changed was on the west side looking across toward the sculpture and the redbud grove. I had Mies van der Rohe-like hedges there before they were removed. This did a lot to spatially define the lawn and define the space."[43]

/ AFTER THE MILLER GARDEN /

For Kiley, the use of the grid, asymmetry, and horizontality represented a radical change in his approach to landscape design [figure 2-24]. After designing the Miller garden, he abandoned the type of free-form, nonorthogonal compositions that he had pursued for nearly nineteen years and embarked on a series of geometric explorations as connections between landscape and architecture. The Air Force Academy of 1956–1968, Dulles Airport of 1958, and a garden for Clarence Hamilton of 1965 clearly illustrate the new ordering principles behind his work. Many architects who shared the vision of a geometrically ordered landscape intimately connected to architecture would select Kiley as collaborator. This commitment to a rigorous, more classical spatial approach is not found in the later designs of Kiley's Harvard contemporaries Garrett Eckbo and James Rose. Their compositions continued to be more open and experimental—referring to contemporary art—and never embraced the classical tradition that appealed to Kiley's sensibility. Certainly a great part of Kiley's success has been that he did not deny the classical language in his work but used its structure to extend modernism's free plan into the landscape.

/ 2-23 /
MILLER GARDEN.
THE ADULT GARDEN
HEDGES AND REDBUD
GROVE, c. 1957.
/ OFFICE OF DAN KILEY /

/ 2-24 /
MILLER GARDEN.
AT SUNRISE.
/ ALAN WARD /

This essay was previously published in Marc Treib, editor, *Modern Landscape Architecture: A Critical Review* (Cambridge, Mass.: MIT Press, 1993).

I would like to thank the many people who contributed to this essay: Dan Kiley, who allowed me to interview him and graciously provided copies of drawings from his archives; Mr. and Mrs. J. Irwin Miller for permission to publish photographs of their garden; Marc Treib, Reuben Rainey, and Richard Wilson for their comments and suggestions on early drafts; Geoffrey and Sarah Middeleer for their assistance with editing; and my colleagues at the University of Virginia.

The drawings included in this essay would not have been possible without the suppport of the University of Virginia Dean's Forum Faculty Research Grant. Except where otherwise noted in the captions, they are drawn after sources used courtesy of the Office of Dan Kiley. Liza Mueller (figures 2-3, 4, 5, 7, 9, 17, 19, 20), Mary Williams (figures 2-1, 8, 10, 11, 12, 18, 22), and Helen Wilson (figures 2-2, 21), graduate students in landscape architecture at the University of Virginia, and Bradford Bellows (figures 2-13, 14, 15, 16), undergraduate in architecture at the University of Virginia, completed the drawings under my supervision.

NOTES

1 Dan Kiley, "Miller Garden," *Process Architecture No. 33, Landscape Design: Works of Dan Kiley* (October 1982), p. 21.

2 Dan Kiley, interview with the author, 1 June 1990.

3 Ibid.

4 Garrett Eckbo, "Outdoors and In: Gardens as Living Space," *Magazine of Art*, 34 (October 1941), pp. 425, 426.

5 Dan Kiley, interview with author, 1 June 1990.

6 The nature of Church's contribution to the design of the project is not completely known.

7 For an interview with Dan Kiley discussing his design for the Nuremburg Trials Courtroom, see Mark Pendergrast, "Trial and Error," *North by Northeast*, 3, no.3 (Winooski, Vermont: Vermont Public Radio, July 1988), pp. 6–9, 24.

8 "The Bones of a New Hampshire Farmhouse Are Retained in This Warm Country Home," *Architectural Forum*, 88 (March 1948), pp. 81–85.

9 For a complete description of this controversy, see Ruth Layton, "St. Louis Riverfront Revisited 1933–1964," *Landscape Architecture* (April 1964), pp. 182–186.

10 This project should not be confused with Kiley's garden for Clarence Hamilton in Columbus, Indiana, completed in 1965.

11 "A House Hidden in the Woods," *Architectural Forum*, 95 (December 1951), pp. 101–107.

12 Edward L. Barnes, "Platform Houses," Architectural Record (October 1956), pp. 205–212.

13 Eero Saarinen, in Aline Saarinen, ed., *Eero Saarinen on His Work* (New Haven: Yale University Press, 1962), p. 6.

14 Peter Papademetriou, "Coming of Age: Eero Saarinen and Modern American Architecture," *Perspecta: 21*, Yale Architectural Journal, p. 120.

15 Reyner Banham, "Neoclassicism," *Encyclopedia of Modern Architecture* (New York: Harry N. Abrams, Inc., 1964), p. 202

16 Papademetriou, "Coming of Age," pp. 128–131.

17 "GM's Industrial Versailles," *Architectural Forum*, 104 (May 1956), pp. 122–128.

18 Juan Pablo Bonta, *An Anatomy of Architectural Interpretation: A Semiotic Review of the Criticism of Mies van der Rohe's Barcelona Pavilion* (Barcelona: Editorial Gustavo Gili, S. A., 1975), pp. 57–58.

19 Dan Kiley, interview with author, 1 June 1990. In this quote "We" refers to himself and Garrett Eckbo.

20 David Spaeth, "Ludwig Mies van der Rohe: A Biographical Essay," *Mies Reconsidered: His Career, Legacy, and Disciples* (New York: The Art Institute of Chicago and Rizzoli International Publications, 1986), pp. 17-18.

21 Garrett Eckbo, *Landscape for Living* (New York: Architectural Record with Duell, Sloan, & Pearce, 1950), p. 178.

22 Ibid., p. 136.

23 Colin Rowe, "Neo-'Classicism' and Modern Architecture I," written 1956–57, first published in *Oppositions 1* (1973), also in Rowe, *The Mathematics of the Ideal Villa and Other Essays* (Cambridge, Mass.: The MIT Press, 1976), p. 120.

24 "A Contemporary Palladian Villa," *Architectural Forum*, 109 (September 1958), pp. 126–131.

25 Dan Kiley, interview with author, 2 June 1990.

26 Dan Kiley wrote of this centrifugal movement in *Process Architecture #33*, "Miller Garden," p. 21.

27 Dan Kiley, "Lecture," in Warren T. Byrd, Jr. and Reuben M. Rainey, eds., *The Work of Dan Kiley: A Dialogue on Design Theory* (Charlottesville: University of Virginia, School of Architecture, 1983), p. 14; reprinted in this book.

28 Philip C. Johnson, *Mies van der Rohe* (New York: The Museum of Modern Art, 1947), p. 58.

29 Kenneth Frampton, "Modernism and Tradition in the Work of Mies van der Rohe, 1920–1968," *Mies Reconsidered*, p. 41.

30 For a description of the importance of Wittkower's book, see Henry A. Millon, "Rudolf Wittkower, Architectural Principles in the Age of Humanism: Its Influence on the Development and Interpretation of Modern Architecture," *Journal of the Society of Architectural Historians* (1972), pp. 83–91.

31 Banham, "Neoclassicism," pp. 204–205.

32 Kenneth Frampton, "Notes on Classical and Modern Themes in the Architecture of Mies van der Rohe and Auguste Perret," *Classical Tradition and the Modern Movement* (Helsinki: Finnish Association of Finnish Architects, Museum of Finnish Architecture, Alvar Aalto Museum, 1985), p. 22.

33 Dan Kiley, "My Design Process," *Process Architecture No. 33*, p. 15.

34 See Kiley, "Panel Discussion," *The Work of Dan Kiley*, p. 30.

35 Joseph Hudnut, "Space in the Modern Garden," in *Architecture and the Spirit of Man* (Cambridge, Mass.: Harvard University Press, 1949), p. 137, quoted by Garrett Eckbo in *Landscape for Living*, p. 61, and reprinted in Christopher Tunnard's *Gardens in the Modern Landscape*, 2d ed. (1948), p. 176. This short essay provides perhaps the clearest description of the "modern" garden as envisioned by Kiley, Eckbo, and Rose.

36 Rosalind E. Krauss, "Grids," in *Originality of the Avant-Garde and Other Modernist Myths* (Cambridge, Mass.: MIT Press, 1985), p. 10.

37 Walter Gropius, "The Theory and Organization of the Bauhaus," in Herbert Bayer, Walter Gropius, and Ise Gropius, eds., *Bauhaus 1919-1928* (New York: The Museum of Modern Art, 1938), p. 30.

38 Dan Kiley, "My Design Process," p. 17.

39 Kenneth Frampton, *Modern Architecture: A Critical History* (London: Thames and Hudson, 1980), p. 164.

40 James Rose, "Freedom in the Garden," *Pencil Points* (October 1938), p. 640.

41 For a complete discussion of de Stijl theory and principles, see H. L. C. Jaffé, *De Stijl 1917–1931* (Cambridge, Mass.: Belknap Press of Harvard University, 1986).

42 Dan Kiley, "Miller Garden," p. 15.

43 Dan Kiley, interview with author, 2 June 1990.

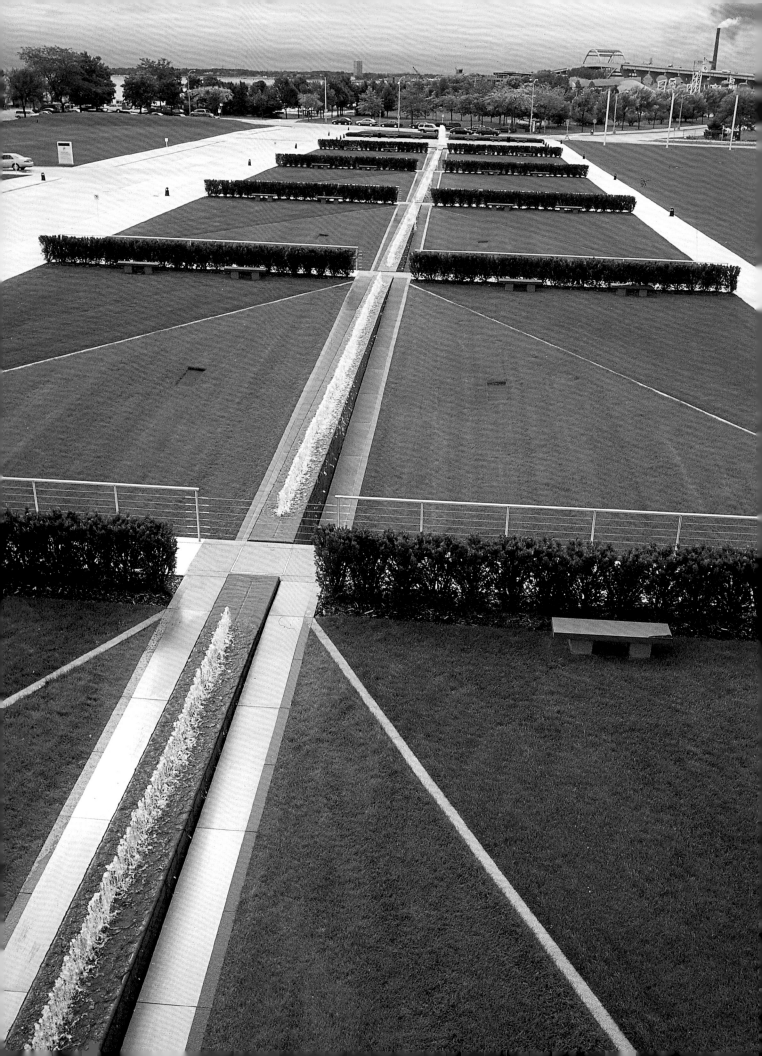

/ 3 /

Dan Kiley in Public

John Beardsley

What can we learn about Dan Kiley's ambitions as a designer from his publications and public utterances? Kiley was famously reticent; he wrote little and seldom spoke on the record in public. Apart from three articles coauthored with James Rose and Garrett Eckbo soon after their student years, the inventory of his publications includes just a one-page essay that appeared in *Landscape Architecture* in 1963; two brief texts a decade apart in *Process Architecture* (1982 and 1993); and a book of his work coauthored with Jane Amidon in 1999. In addition, Kiley consented to a couple of published interviews. Often when he did write or speak, the content was more personal and anecdotal than theoretical or interpretive; the paucity of his recorded remarks is one reason his lecture at the First Annual Symposium on Landscape Architecture at the University of Virginia in February 1982 is so worthy of re-publication: It provides one of the few clear statements available to us of Kiley's design philosophy, supplemented by his comments in the discussion that followed.

As rare as they are, however, Kiley's published writings provide a valuable entry into the world of his ideas. His first recorded thoughts appear in the essays composed with Rose and Eckbo, titled "Landscape Design in the Urban Environment," "Landscape Design in the Rural Environment," and "Landscape Design in the Primeval Environment," which appeared in the May and August 1939 and February 1940 issues of *Architectural Record*. Eckbo and Rose were both far more prolific writers than Kiley; we know from his statements at the Virginia symposium that they carried most of the weight in composing these texts. But the essays convey several ideas that undergird Kiley's own subsequent writings. Foremost is the idea conveyed in the titles that landscape architecture can and should operate at a variety of scales [figure 3-1]. Another major concept is that landscapes of different types need to be in balance. As they wrote in the essay

/ 3-1 /

DAN KILEY, CUDAHY GARDENS, MILWAUKEE, WISCONSIN, 2002.

THIS FRONTISPIECE TO THE MILWAUKEE MUSEUM OF ART WAS ONE OF KILEY'S LAST REALIZED WORKS.

/ MARC TREIB /

on the primeval environment, "Now—with a population largely concentrated in or near an urban environment—the problem becomes one of establishing and then controlling an environmental equilibrium—urban, rural, primeval." At every scale, the essays suggest, design should address the specific needs of local populations, whether human, animal, or vegetal: "As all design of the urban environment is based primarily on the needs of the city dweller, and that of the rural environment on the inhabitants of the country, any intelligent planning of the primeval must be based on *the needs of its native 'population'—beasts, birds, insects, and plant life.*"[1] In large measure, the landscape is presented in these texts from the perspective of its modes of production: the urban as an expression of industry; the rural as an expression of agriculture. The main focus of the essays is on devising systems of recreation appropriate to the social patterns of each landscape type.

The essays are shot through with modernist assumptions: that the orchestration of volumetric space is the designer's primary mode of expression; that landscapes should be functional, flexible, and adapted to the patterns of contemporary life, including mobility and mechanization; and that they ought to employ new materials and techniques of production. As the authors wrote in the essay on landscape design in the urban environment, "The approach has shifted, as in building, from the grand manner of axes and façades to specific needs and specific forms to address those needs." Their emphasis is more on how landscapes function than on how they look: their goal, they say, is to "achieve volumes of organized space in which people live and play, rather than stand and look." But the authors suggest that modernism involved transformations in ideology

as well as in practice: "Landscape design is going through the same reconstruction in ideology and method that has changed every other form of planning since the industrial revolution." Ideological changes included liberation from design conventions, especially those of the Beaux-Arts, and the freedom to serve a variety of social groups, not merely the elite. In the essay on the urban environment, for instance, they insist that "the urban dweller requires a complete, evenly distributed, and flexible system providing all types of recreation for persons of every age, interest, and sex."[2] They conceive of landscape architecture as a social practice with a scientific, even ecological, basis: in the essay on the primeval environment, they argue for "the biological conception of environmental design as found in scientific agriculture and as exemplified by the life cycle and group habits found in many of the lower organisms."[3]

But there are striking differences between these essays and Kiley's subsequent writings: they are enumerative and discursive, while Kiley's tend to be intuitive and terse—even aphoristic. Perhaps more importantly, they are short on commentary about the emotional and spiritual dimensions of contact with nature, which appears often in Kiley's own texts. This quality is foreshadowed in a brief and somewhat anomalous paragraph in "Landscape Design in the Urban Environment," which reads in part: "Every individual has a certain optimum space relation—that is, he requires a certain volume of space around him for the greatest contentment and development of body and soul . . . This need falls into the intangible group of invisible elements in human life which have been largely disregarded in the past. Privacy out-of-doors means relaxation, emotional release from

contact, reunion with nature and the soil."[4] These sorts of sentiments—with their almost Transcendentalist overtones —are far more pervasive in the texts Kiley subsequently composed himself.

Kiley's independent voice, first heard in "Nature: The Source of All Design," published in the January 1963 issue of *Landscape Architecture*, reiterates some of the assumptions evident in the essays written with Eckbo and Rose. He argues for total environmental design, especially through the integration of landscape and architecture; he defines landscape design as "the organization of space to satisfy certain human functions." At the same time, he articulates ambitions beyond function. Notable is a notion that design is an expression of values: "in projecting a design, one is stating one's position, describing one's philosophy, explaining one's values." The values he articulates include a "thirst for organization and discipline"; tellingly, he describes spatial organization as "a freeing process, a release of the spirit through the simplification of organization in continuity." He critiques the modernist application of pattern—curves, diamonds, kidney-shapes—without an appreciation of their spatial consequences and without an awareness of their relevance to natural processes: "We are still concerned with form rather than process. We are not searching for form; forms are results of the nature of process... In landscape design, one does not copy nature but tries to understand underlying processes or workings of nature—it is all there. Man as part of nature, not man and nature." Above all, it appears, Kiley aims for an expression of human life entirely integrated with nature: "In my own work, I always am excited with the idea of man as clearly recognizable in nature—projecting

his designs in clear strength and letting the natural land-scape lap its shores, or modifying and breaking it up until total assimilation has taken place" [figure 3-2].[5]

While we can recognize in this text some fundamental attributes of modernist thinking—the emphasis on func-tionality, on spatial organization, and on freedom from traditional structural and compositional constraints—its greater significance lies in its suspicion of purely formal strategies, combined with what we might recognize from more current discourse as an emphasis on natural processes. A similar combination is evident in Kiley's first essay for *Process Architecture* (1982), where he reiterates his quest for freedom and wholeness, for simplicity and clarity generated by site and function, modified by an understanding of the natural landscape. He describes his design process in terms that are part functional, part poetic: "Design aims to solve functional problems, not create forms and patterns which are ends in themselves." At the same time, he says, "design describes that process of discovery through which the form becomes known." Again, he conceptualizes design as the orchestration of dynamic process: "One sets the design in motion and it makes its own growth; [an] organism continually in a state of dynamic equilibrium trying to find its place in the universe." In landscape architecture at every scale, he says, "the objective is the integration of man and nature into one."[6]

The attitude to history evident in this essay confounds a widespread assumption that modernists were indifferent or even hostile to the past: "My education of the landscape consists importantly of knowledge and experience of historical gardens and places, which continually expose

/ **3-2** /
DAN KILEY, CURRIER FARM,
DANBY, VERMONT, 1959.
/ ALAN WARD /

creative and beautiful ways human needs have been accommodated." Here, as elsewhere, Kiley cites the importance of classic French gardens such as Villandry, which provided him with an organizational vocabulary at once geometric and productive—both in the agricultural sense and in the construction of cultural identity [see figure C-4]. He also acknowledges the importance to him of traditional Japanese design—but less the gardens than the houses, which he found more satisfying in his quest for organization and discipline: "It is the Japanese house which excites me and influences my design with its ordering of continuous interpenetrating spaces into a serviceable and unified whole" [figure 3-3].[7] He also makes passing reference to the importance of philosophers and even a psychologist in his approach to design: Emerson, Thoreau, Goethe, and Jung.

Kiley's reference to the Transcendentalists Emerson and Thoreau prompts the question: What did he mean by nature? As a modernist, he was in part a man of science, as suggested in this essay by his characterization of nature as "man's ecological source." He likewise reiterates an idea that nature is a productive system: man is "dependent on it for his livelihood," which is expressed in Kiley's life-long affection for the organized landscape of fields, canals, allées, and gridded groves. The productive landscape became one of his primary sources of design precedent.[8] Kiley presents both nature itself and the experience of nature as dynamic: in the second of his *Process Architecture* essays (1993), he says: "Every time you walk in nature it is a fresh experience. Whether you squeeze through a small opening in the maple trees, pick your way across a rushing stream, or climb a hill to discover an open meadow,

/ **3-3** /
SHOKIN-TEI, KATSURA VILLA, KYOTO, JAPAN, 17th CENTURY.
/ MARC TREIB /
/ **3-4** /
DAN KILEY, AG CORPORATION, BRUSSELS, BELGIUM, 1993.
/ MARC TREIB /

everything is always moving and changing spatially." Perhaps most importantly, nature is conceptualized in philosophical, even spiritual, terms: in the second *Process* essay he affirms that "we are all part of the universe, inextricably part of the whole." Design, he says, "should relate outwardly to a context, but should also explode spatially—to the infinite." Kiley insists in this essay that "the greatest contribution the landscape designer can make" is "to link the human and the natural in such a way as to recall our fundamental place in the scheme of things" [figure 3-4].[9]

Kiley's remarks at the 1982 University of Virginia symposium deepen our understanding of his philosophical positions [figure 3-5]. We should not be surprised that, as a New Englander educated in the early decades of the twentieth century, Kiley made much of both Olmsted and the Transcendentalists. He begins by attributing to Thoreau the source of his ambition to live lightly on the earth; he then ratifies an idea he derived from Olmsted about "aptness"—the idea that design ought to be appropriate to its context. (This may well have been an allusion to the debate that Olmsted conducted with Mariana Van Rensselaer about her essay "Architectural Fitness," which appeared initially in *Garden and Forest* in August 1891 and was collected two years later in her book *Art Out-of-Doors*; both her essay and Olmsted's rebuttal were reprinted in the May 1973 issue of the *Journal of the Society of Architectural Historians*).[10] Kiley goes on to embrace Emerson's notion of the "whole man," which he uses as a way of explaining his effort to bring his domestic and professional lives together on his farm in Charlotte, Vermont [figure 3-6].

/ **3-5** /
THE WORK OF DAN KILEY:
A DIALOGUE ON DESIGN
THEORY,
SCHOOL OF ARCHITECTURE,
UNIVERSITY OF VIRGINIA,
1982. COVER.

Kiley affirms in this text that he was inspired by Emerson "very much from the beginning" by "a beautiful essay called 'The Whole Man'." While not actually the title of a discrete text, the notion of "the whole man" was invoked in some of Emerson's most familiar essays. In "The American Scholar," for instance, it is used in a discussion of human occupations, which Emerson thought were divided to facilitate social life, much as the fingers are separated to enhance dexterity. But this leads to a fragmentation of individual existence: "Man is priest, and scholar, and statesman, and producer, and soldier. In the divided or social state, these functions are parcelled out to individuals, each of whom aims to do his stint of the joint work, whilst each other performs his... The state of society is one in which the members have suffered amputation from the trunk, and strut about so many walking monsters, —a good finger, a neck, a stomach, an elbow, but never a man." Ever the idealist—if a qualified one—Emerson sought to restore the essential wholeness of existence through the reintegration of the parts of man: "there is One Man,—present to all particular men only partially, or through one faculty; ... you must take the whole society to find the whole man. Man is not a farmer, or a professor, or an engineer, but he is all."[11]

This notion reappears in an essay from Emerson's First Series entitled "Compensation," in the context of a discussion of how the entire universe is represented in each one of its particles: "The world globes itself in a drop of dew," as he put it succinctly. Then he elaborated:

Every thing in nature contains all the powers of nature. Every thing is made of one hidden stuff; as the naturalist sees one type under every metamorphosis,

*and regards a horse as a running man, a fish as a
swimming man, a bird as a flying man, a tree as
a rooted man. Each new form repeats not only the
main character of the type, but part for part all
the details, all the aims, furtherances, hindrances,
energies, and whole system of every other. Every
occupation, trade, art, transaction, is a compend
of the world, and a correlative of every other. Each
one is an entire emblem of human life; of its good
and ill, its trials, its enemies, its course and its end.
And each one must somehow accommodate the whole
man, and recite all his destiny.*[12]

This is Emerson at perhaps his most relevant to Kiley,
articulating the precepts that would motivate the designer:
that we are inextricably—even mystically—part of nature;
that everything we do is part of some larger order and
radiates out to the universe; and that we must unify the
fragmented parts of our existences to approach the condition of wholeness. "We are one with the universe," the
Emersonian Kiley proclaims in his University of Virginia
remarks.[13]

The Virginia text cites other more pragmatic influences
—Warren Manning, for instance, for whom Kiley worked
in the early 1930s, just out of high school, and whom he
described as "a philosopher of the land ... who helped
establish many of the early parks." And Kiley here singles
out the importance to him of André Le Nôtre, whose work
he first encountered on a trip to Europe in 1945, when—
as chief of the design section of the Office of Strategic
Services—he oversaw the reconstruction of the bombed-
out Palace of Justice in Nuremberg, which included
designing courtrooms for the trials of Nazi war criminals.

He recalls being especially impressed by Le Nôtre's landscape
at the Château de Sceaux, which he celebrates for spatial
sequences that result from simplicity, organization, and
symmetry—qualities he also recognized in olive groves
near Cordoba, Spain, where grids of trees planted on 30-
foot centers are transformed by variations in topography.
Kiley's embrace of the qualities of Le Nôtre's designs led
many—including the designer himself—to characterize
Kiley as a classicist, but he typically took the familiar
elements of the classical landscape—bosques, allées, axes,
bilateral symmetry—and improvised upon them, changing their function or orientation, even dispersing them in
asymmetrical ways.

The University of Virginia text is not the last time we
encounter Kiley the philosopher. The book written with Jane
Amidon borrows liberally from his previous writings; the
Transcendentalist Kiley finds expression in a section called
"Philosophy," where the designer once again asserts the
interconnectedness of all life. "I am always searching for
the purest connection to that which holds us all together,"
he affirms. "We can call it spirit or mystery; it can be
embodied by descriptions of the universe or of religion;
it takes the form of sacred geometries and infinitesimal
ecologies. There is an evolving, ever-changing, many-faceted
order that binds everything into harmonious parts of the
greater whole." Design, he insists, is not some autonomous
discipline, but part of an integrated life. Echoing his
interpretation of "the whole man," he says, "The thing
that's important is not something called design; it's how
you live, it's life itself. Design really comes from that. You
cannot separate what you do from your life."[14]

/ **3-6** /
**KILEY OFFICE,
CHARLOTTE VERMONT.**
/ MARC TREIB, 1991 /

How effective was Kiley in translating these public utterances into public landscapes? At the most apparent level, Kiley's public work manifests a belief in the capacity of geometry to organize landscape at a variety of scales; it likewise demonstrates a reliable emphasis on functionalism and aptness to program. Both through the use of a limited number of elements and by their extrapolation into space, he aimed consistently for an expression of his notion of the liberation of simplicity—the "release of the spirit through the simplicity of organization in continuity," as he put it. Although the garden was at the heart of his practice, and although the garden and the institutional landscape were the locus of his most successful and—not coincidentally —best preserved work, he regularly sought to apply these principles in the public landscape.

Indeed, Kiley was powerfully motivated by democratic impulses in his early years. After leaving Harvard in 1938, he moved to Washington, D.C., to work on public housing, partially as an employee of the United States Housing Authority (1939–41) and partially as a consultant to Louis Kahn.[15] Inducted into the Army in 1942, Kiley spent the war years with the Army Corps of Engineers and then the Office of Strategic Services. After the war, he threw himself into public projects: he was a member of Eero Saarinen's winning team for the design of the Jefferson National Expansion Memorial in St Louis in 1947; this project was followed about a decade later by his designs for the U.S. Air Force Academy in Colorado Springs, on which he worked with Skidmore, Owings, and Merrill from 1956 to 1968 [figures 3-8, 3-9]. In between, he designed over ninety gardens (few of which were actually implemented) for a suburban Virginia housing development called Hollin Hills, part of the postwar boom in housing to accommodate returning veterans.[16]

Several projects from the 1960s stand out for the clarity with which they express Kiley's public ambitions. His work on the Third Block of Independence Mall in Philadelphia, for instance (1963), reveals both his confidence in the organizing power of geometry and his attention to historical context. The final block of a three-block sequence stretching north from Independence Hall, the project was intended as a place of rest for visitors to the area's historic sites. Kiley conceived of the space as an "architectural forest," basing the design on the original layout of Philadelphia by Thomas Holme, William Penn's surveyor. The city was laid out on a grid with a central square for city hall and four squares located symmetrically around it; Kiley used that module three times in the Third Block of Independence Mall. He located three primary fountains on the central axis and set smaller fountains out from their corners to form a quincunx. A tightly-spaced grid of honey-locust trees— selected for their delicate foliage, graceful branching, and hardiness in urban conditions—was devised to unify the space; planted on a 12-by-18-foot module in brick pavers, the 700 trees formed a spatial mass out of which the fountain squares and some subsidiary open spaces were cut. The trees formed a rhythm of open and closed space, or "dilation and contraction," as Kiley put it: "from one point of reference, one can move outwards into the cosmos or just as easily inwards, into increasingly intimate models of physical or spiritual experience [figures 3-10 to 3-12]."[17] (In this thought, Kiley evokes the 1968 film by Charles and Ray Eames called *Powers of Ten*, which explored similarities in natural patterns from inside the body to

/ **3-7** /
**ANDRÉ LE NÔTRE,
CHÂTEAU DE CHANTILLY,
FRANCE, LATE 17th
CENTURY. THE GARDENS.**
/ MARC TREIB /

/ **3-8** /
JEFFERSON NATIONAL
EXPANSION MEMORIAL,
ST. LOUIS, MISSOURI, 1947.
RENDERING.
/ OFFICE OF DAN KILEY /

/ **3-9** /
UNITED STATES
AIR FORCE ACADEMY,
COLORADO SPRINGS,
COLORADO, 1957–1968.
/ MARC TREIB /

interstellar space.) Kiley visualizes the grid in this instance as expressive of the structure that unifies creation at all scales, from the microcosm to the universe.

Time has not been kind to this project. The site was to have been framed by lines of evergreen shrubs and cedar trees that were never planted; they might have given the block more coherence. Technical difficulties resulted from site conditions: because the subsurface fill was very porous, a clay layer was placed above it to prevent excess drainage. But the clay compacted, causing the opposite problem: too much water, which resulted in leaf wilt and root disintegration. Moreover, the roots that did survive had nowhere to go, so they lifted and dislodged the pavers. Still more, the design was plagued with programmatic and urban planning mistakes not of its own making: Kiley was instructed to extend a central axis from the first and second blocks of Independence Mall into the third block, creating a long vista that was vastly out of scale with Independence Hall at its far end. In addition, neither the historic context nor the interpretive program extended into the third block, so the space was essentially without function. Compounding these problems, the site was surrounded by the U.S. Mint and other large buildings that presented blank façades to the street; there were no shops or restaurants to animate the perimeter of the project, which made it attractive to vagrants. Neglect compounded these inherent problems; by the 1990s, Kiley's design was doomed. Called in to devise a new plan for the site in 1997, Laurie Olin recognized it was hopeless to try to salvage the project: "Could Kiley's design have been reused in our plan? No, because the program to repair the gash in the city caused by the park in the first place (several hundred buildings were demolished to create it) called for putting back urban fabric, namely buildings with active façades and visitors... I, too, came to the conclusion that Dan's park was ruined, and that if rebuilt it would fail again because it was a serious urban planning mistake that weakened the Penn plan and the city, not a landscape design one."[18] The Third Block is now the site of the National Constitution Center, a museum devoted to the nation's founding documents, which occupies almost the entire site.

Kiley's design for Dulles International Airport near Washington, D.C. (1963) has fared only slightly better: much of it is gone now, replaced by enormous parking structures. Yet the original design reveals Kiley's emphasis on function and aptness to program: circulation is paramount; this is a landscape of roads and parking. The design also put to the test his idea of "man as clearly recognizable in nature—projecting his designs in clear strength and letting the natural landscape lap its shores, or modifying and breaking it up until total assimilation has taken place." Again, Kiley devised a lucid spatial structure using repeated modules, deploying the plants of the Virginia countryside in lines and grids to evoke the hedges and windrows of the original agricultural context [figures 3-13 to 3-15]. Kiley conceived of the below-grade parking lot in front of Eero Saarinen's powerfully sculptural terminal as a vast entry court; it was set in an ellipse that was to be framed at either end by double rows of tulip poplar trees, with a triple row across from the terminal. Tulip poplars attain great stature; they were intended to balance the soaring roof of the building. (They were subsequently changed to somewhat-less-grand red oaks.)

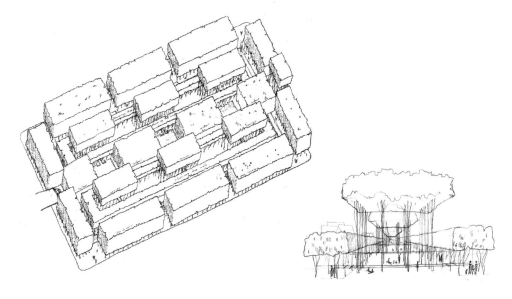

Lines of London plane trees divided sections of the parking; the ellipse was edged with grids of firethorn, with rows of red oak and groves of red cedar on 20-foot centers beyond. Kiley's notion was that these elements would mediate between the building and the surrounding countryside, diminishing in scale and density as they got farther from the terminal, achieving his goal of being at once clearly recognizable, yet assimilated with nature. Much of his original planting plan has been obliterated by the new parking garages.

Kiley's emphasis on function as generator of form is evident in another infrastructural project from the same years, the Chicago Filtration Plant of 1965 [figure 3-16]. A 61-acre constructed landfill adjacent to the Navy Pier, the site includes filtration reservoirs, laboratories, offices, and pump rooms, along with a 10-acre public park. The site's character is beautifully and simply expressed in five pools of different sizes scattered irregularly in the park like an extinguished constellation—or like stones in a Japanese garden, as Kiley insisted. Set in low mounds that are carefully graded, the pools are ringed with 20-foot-wide bands of concrete that step down to the water; they range in diameter from 90 to 200 feet, their scale evoking the infrastructural functions of the adjacent plant. In Kiley's mind, they also symbolized the five Great Lakes; we might also recognize in them an asymmetrical echo of Le Nôtre's water parterres [see figure 3-7].[19] Extremely exposed to wind and cold in the winter and heat in the summer, the park demanded hearty plant material. A grove of informally-massed honey-locusts marks the entry to the site, creating a buffer between park and city; rows of the same tree continue along the promenade and bike

/ **3-12** / *opposite above*
DAN KILEY,
THIRD BLOCK, INDEPENDENCE
MALL, PHILADELPHIA,
PENNSYLVANIA, 1963.
/ REUBEN RAINEY /

/ **3-13** / *opposite below*
DAN KILEY,
LANDSCAPE ARCHITECT;
EERO SAARINEN,
ARCHITECT;
DULLES AIRPORT,
CHANTILLY, VIRGINIA, 1963.
VIEW OVER THE PARKING
AREAS SHORTLY AFTER
PLANTING.
/ ALAN WARD /

/ **3-14** / *above*
DULLES AIRPORT.
LINES OF PYRACANTHUS
IN GRACEFUL CURVES.
/ REUBEN RAINEY /

/ **3-15** / *below*
DULLES AIRPORT.
/ REUBEN RAINEY, 1983 /

path that rings the promontory—interrupted at regular intervals to create a condition of exposure and enclosure, or "dilation and contraction," as Kiley put it in the case of the Independence Mall project. Lower-growing hawthorns are used around seating areas; barberry is planted on some slopes near the water [figure 3-17]. This is one of Kiley's most imposing civic landscapes; it uses metaphors of the water filtration process to generate its language of form, underscoring Kiley's idea that "design aims to solve functional problems, not create forms and patterns which are ends in themselves."

Kiley's work for cultural institutions also resulted in the creation of significant civic spaces that confirmed his design principles. At Lincoln Center in New York, for example, he contributed to the creation of a campus of performing arts institutions, designing a one-acre court in 1960 that conveys his trademark "simplicity of organization in continuity." Oriented around an 80-by-120-foot pool, the space was framed on two sides by 20-by-20-foot plant boxes, a double row of six each to the south and a single row of six to the east. Coordinated with the plaza's paving module, the planting boxes were necessitated by the fact that the site is over a parking garage. The boxes were originally planted with a tightly-spaced quartet of London plane trees, which were closely clipped to create a vegetative mass that would assume an architectural character and hold its own against the buildings. Ultimately, these trees—four to a box—were replaced by a single pear tree in each, which destroyed the scale relationship between planters and buildings. The entire project has now been demolished.

More recently, at the Nelson-Atkins Museum in Kansas City, Kiley created a 22-acre sculpture park that doubles

/ **3-16** /
DAN KILEY,
WATER FILTRATION PLANT,
CHICAGO. ILLINOIS, 1965.
AERIAL VIEW.
THE PLAY OF GEOMETRIC
SHAPES RECALLS LE NÔTRE'S
DESIGN FOR THE FRENCH
CHÂTEAU OF CHANTILLY.
/ FLL, HGSD /

/ **3-17** /
WATER FILTRATION PLANT.
LAKESHORE PROMENADE.
/ FLL, HGSD /

as a great forecourt for the museum's 1933 Beaux-Arts building [figure 3-18]. Working with architect Jaquelin Robertson, Kiley recontoured the sloping site, creating five grass-covered terraces that step down from the building's south façade, alternating with slopes of Japanese yew [figure 3-19]. A staggered double line of ginkgos was planted on each terrace. Selected because their upright habit would leave ample space for the sculptures beneath, the ginkgos are interrupted at the center to create an axial vista aligned with the building's portico. At the base of the terraces is a broad lawn framed by Redmond lindens (a hearty species developed in nearby Nebraska) planted in quincunx patterns. To either side, the geometry breaks down in a rolling landscape with serpentine pathways and more irregular plantings, in another evocation of Kiley's principle of projecting design "in clear strength and letting the natural landscape lap its shores, or modifying and breaking it up until total assimilation has taken place" [figure 3-20]. Completed in 1989, this remains one of Kiley's most carefully conceived and executed landscapes, and one of his better preserved public projects—notwithstanding the addition of Steven Holl's handsome and luminous pavilions, which extend the museum's facilities along the eastern edge of the park. The project also underlines some of the distinctions between Kiley's private and institutional landscapes. There is typically greater transparency in his public than in his private projects—higher tree canopies and lower hedges, for instance, which imply enclosure without closure—whereas his private gardens can seem more sealed off.

Perhaps we should not be surprised that many of Kiley's public projects have been destroyed or changed beyond

recognition. Design, as Kiley knew, expresses values; as he also knew, those values change. Landscape architecture continues to undergo, in the words of Kiley, Eckbo, and Rose, "the same reconstruction in ideology and method that has changed every other form of planning since the industrial revolution." Some of these transformations in ideology and method have challenged Kiley's particular values: for instance, his quest for simplification—his "thirst for organization and discipline"—has given way to a growing interest in complexity science and chaos theory; his view of nature as a productive system has yielded in some measure to a conception of nature as dynamic, contingent, imperiled, even catastrophic—subject to both human and natural disturbance. But it is Kiley's Transcendentalist rhetoric that might be most in retreat. His notion that "we are one with the universe," that we are harmonious parts of a greater whole that can be spoken of in terms of spirit or mystery sounds increasingly foreign in an overwhelmingly secular and pragmatic age.

But there is still much to admire in Kiley's rhetoric, even if his best ideas are not always evident in the designs themselves—at least in the more public ones. Still particularly relevant, I think, is his assertion that "one does not copy nature but tries to understand underlying processes or workings of nature." This notion is consistent with some of the current principles of ecological design—although, in Kiley's almost reflexive attachment to rational geometry, his complaint that "we are still concerned with form rather than process" could apply to his own work as much as anyone's. We can still laud his engagement with infrastructure and urban systems more generally, along with his emphasis on spatial perception, on the insight

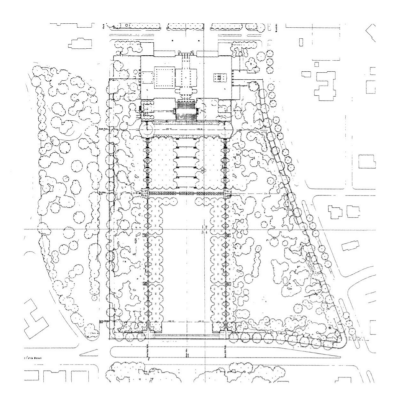

/ **3-18** / *opposite above*
DAN KILEY,
LANDSCAPE ARCHITECT;
JAQUELIN ROBERTSON,
ARCHITECT;
HENRY MOORE SCULPTURE
GARDEN, NELSON-ATKINS
MUSEUM, KANSAS CITY,
MISSOURI, 1988. SITE PLAN.
/ OFFICE OF DAN KILEY /

/ **3-19** / *opposite below*
HENRY MOORE SCULPTURE
GARDEN, KANSAS CITY,
MISSOURI.
/ MARC TREIB /

/ **3-20** / *below*
HENRY MOORE SCULPTURE
GARDEN, KANSAS CITY,
MISSOURI.
LINES OF GINKGOS ANCHOR
THE TERRACES.
/ MARC TREIB /

that nature and our experience of nature are dynamic: "everything is always moving and changing spatially." Trenchant too is his conviction that culture and nature— for better or for worse—are inextricably intertwined. And it might be time to recuperate, as a basis for a renewed metaphysics of design, his belief that created landscapes can link us to something larger than ourselves and inspire the liberation of the spirit in nature. Kiley inherited from Emerson and Thoreau and continued to profess a notion that spirit was immanent in nature and that contact with landscape was emotionally and spiritually uplifting. Despite the overwhelmingly practical, social, and technological ambitions of modernism, this was a conviction he shared with some of his contemporaries, notably Luis Barragan. As Kiley noted in the book he wrote with Jane Amidon, "Luis Barragan once said that 'beauty speaks like an oracle, and man has heeded its message in an infinite number of ways...a garden must combine the poetic and the mysterious with serenity and joy.' It is the mystic and the beautiful that we seek to attain through revealing our place in the order of Nature."[20] Admittedly, Kiley's language could be maddeningly non-specific, even evasive. Read critically, his ideas might be characterized as a degraded modernist formulation of the philosophical positions he inherited. Read more charitably, however, his words might suggest a way beyond an excessively pragmatic and even secularized present. Indeed, as his public designs are lost, Kiley might become increasingly important as a thinker, as lean as his writings are. "It is all there."

/ **3-21** /
DAN KILEY,
LANDSCAPE ARCHITECT;
I.M. PEI & PARTNERS,
ARCHITECTS;
FOUNTAIN PLACE,
DALLAS, TEXAS, 1985.
/ MARC TREIB /

NOTES

1 Quotations in this paragraph from Garrett Eckbo, Daniel U. Kiley, and James C. Rose, "Landscape Design in the Primeval Environment," *Architectural Record* (February 1940). reprinted in Marc Treib, ed. *Modern Landscape Architecture: A Critical Review* (Cambridge, Mass.: MIT Press, 1993), pp. 88, 89.

2 Preceding quotations from Eckbo, Kiley, and Rose, "Landscape Design in the Urban Environment," *Architectural Record* (May 1939), reprinted in Treib, *Modern Landscape Architecture*, pp. 82, 79.

3 Eckbo, Kiley, Rose, "Landscape Design in the Primeval Environment," in *Modern Landscape Architecture*, p. 91.

4 Eckbo, Kiley, Rose, "Landscape Design in the Urban Environment," in *Modern Landscape Architecture*, p. 80.

5 Quotations in this paragraph from Dan Kiley, "Nature: The Source of All Design," *Landscape Architecture* (January 1963), p. 127.

6 Quotations in this paragraph from Dan Kiley, "My Design Process," *Process Architecture No. 33, Landscape Design of Dan Kiley* (October 1982), pp. 16, 15, 18, 19.

7 "My Design Process," pp. 16, 17.

8 Ibid., pp. 15, 20.

9 Dan Kiley, "What is Design?" *Dan Kiley: Landscape Design II, In Step With Nature, Process Architecture #108* (1993), pp. 10, 8.

10 Cynthia Zaitzevsky, "The Olmsted Firm and the Structures of the Boston Park System," *Journal of the Society of Architectural Historians*, 32 (May 1973), pp. 167–174. The substance of their argument revolved around Van Rensselaer's assertion that Olmsted's structures in the Back Bay Fens, Boston, were too rude or rustic and thus unfit for an urban park;
Olmsted retorted that the project was not intended to be an urban park, but a catchment basin for dirty water and "the restoration to decency of a tract of degraded fen-land, about which a city was threatening to grow" (p. 170).

11 Ralph Waldo Emerson, "The American Scholar" (1837), in Brooks Atkinson, ed., *The Selected Writings of Ralph Waldo Emerson* (New York: The Modern Library, 1968), p. 46.

12 Emerson, "Compensation," from *Essays: First Series* (1841), in *Selected Writings*, pp. 174–175. Emerson's qualified idealism is most evident in the "noble doubt" passage in Section IV, "Idealism," of *Nature* (1836), in *Selected Writings*, p. 26.

13 Kiley's enthusiasm for the Emersonian idea of the whole man may help to shed some light on his interest in Jung, whom he mentions both in the first *Process Architecture* publication and in his comments at the Virginia symposium. Particularly relevant to Kiley might have been Jung's method of "analytical psychology," which addressed itself as much to creative potential as to neurosis, with a goal of integrating conscious and unconscious forces to achieve a meaningful wholeness of life. Kiley might also have perceived analogies between Emerson's belief in the mystical unity of all creation and Jung's notion of a "collective unconscious" common to all humanity and containing universal archetypal symbols. However, Kiley did not attempt to embody any specific Jungian archetypal symbolism in his work; at least he never acknowledged in his writings or spoken comments any ambition to do so.

14 Dan Kiley and Jane Amidon, *Dan Kiley in His Own Words: America's Master Landscape Architect* (London: Thames and Hudson, 1999), p. 8.

15 Kiley's early work is the subject of Anita Berrizbeitia's essay "Early Housing Projects and Garden Prototypes, 1941-52" in William S. Saunders, ed., *Daniel Urban Kiley: The Early Gardens* (New York: Princeton Architectural Press, 1999), pp. 21–36.

16 These gardens are the subject of two texts in *Daniel Urban Kiley: The Early Gardens*: Daniel Donovan's "The Hundred Gardens: The Social, Historical, and Design Contexts of Hollin Hills," pp. 37-46, and Mark Klopfer's "Theme and Variation at Hollin Hills: A Typological Investigation," pp. 47–64.

17 *Dan Kiley in His Own Words*, p. 43.

18 Laurie Olin, "Preserve Some, Yes, But also Improve, Add to, and Let Some Go," paper delivered at The Cultural Landscape Foundation's Wave Hill Conference, "Preserving Modern Landscape Architecture and Making Post-War Design Visible," available on line through the Cultural Landscape Foundation website, http://www.tclf.org/pubs_modern.htm

19 Kiley's reference to the five Great Lakes is found in *Process Architecture #33*, p. 122.

20 *Dan Kiley in His Own Words*, p. 14.

/ 4 /

Kiley and the Spaces of Landscape Modernism

Elizabeth K. Meyer

I took the liberty of showing your syllabus to Dan. He wants to make sure you will be talking in 3 dimensions when you get to him. He was also curious about where you were getting your information for your lectures. And he thinks some book (he didn't say which) by Bruno Zevi was important to include in a reading list about modern landscape architecture... Dan thinks his work—simple as it is—transcends these stylistic quirks—and makes space the most important thing.
Letter from Anne Corcoran to Beth Meyer,
15 February 1983

/ INTRODUCTION /

Twenty-five years ago I taught a course on Landscape Architecture Modernism. I was a year out of graduate school and had a one-year Visiting Lecturer appointment at Cornell's College of Art, Architecture and Planning. It was the first time I had taught such a class. I had never even taken such a class. Such was the state of American landscape architectural education in the 1970s and early 1980s. Having taken several courses in architectural history and theory, I knew the century between the careers of two seminal figures in my profession, Frederick Law Olmsted, Sr. and Ian McHarg, was a momentous one in architecture. And having spent untold time in libraries at the University of Virginia and Cornell University during my four years as a graduate student, I had perused dozens of books by and about twentieth-century American and European landscape architects. This class at Cornell was my first opportunity to collect that reading, until then only synthesized in a few graduate seminar papers and a short lecture at the Virginia AIA annual meeting, into a semester-long inquiry with a small group of graduate students.[1]

Just before the semester began, I sent my Cornell course syllabus to Anne Corcoran asking for her comments and advice. Anne was a friend from graduate school who was also interested in modernist landscapes; her route to learning more about the topic led her to Vermont and the office of Dan Kiley. Anne's response confirmed my sense of Kiley's contributions to the discourse of landscape architecture modernism. He saw three-dimensional space as his medium, and wanted me to understand it, to explain it through writings such as Bruno Zevi's *Towards an Organic Architecture* (1945,1950) or *Architecture as Space* (1948, 1957). Anne's hand-written notes are still in my manila folder labeled "Dan Kiley—Miscellany" after twenty-five years, seven moves, and two decades of

/ 4-0 /
DAN KILEY,
LANDSCAPE ARCHITECT;
EERO SAARINEN,
ARCHITECT;
MILLER GARDEN AND HOUSE,
COLUMBUS, INDIANA, 1955.
/ MARC TREIB /

teaching courses about theories and practices of modern landscape architecture at Harvard and the University of Virginia, reminding me how I decided upon this particular interpretation, this particular theoretical lens through which to introduce Kiley to my graduate students.

The spatial focus of my course lecture on Kiley's gardens and public landscapes is commonplace today and pervades the literature on Kiley that has been written since Byrd and Rainey's Kiley symposium at the University of Virginia in 1982.[2] I attended that symposium as a graduate student and remember feeling I was witnessing the rediscovery of this man's work that was long overshadowed by McHargian environmentalism. Especially memorable was Kiley's response when Laurie Olin asked him about the "relation-ships of formal geometry" that defined his modernism. Kiley never mentioned geometry. Rather he spoke passion-ately of the "poetics of space, where space is continuous; where two-dimensional space gets broken down into a movement—dynamic movement that never ends, but extends into infinity. Movement that is ever-continuous and elusive, like a maze." Kiley went on to praise Le Nôtre, "the Victorians," Frank Lloyd Wright, and Jefferson, as each created places that evoked strong spatial experiences.[3]

The recent scholarly writing on Kiley's work by Amidon, Berrizbeitia, Bleam, Donovan, Hilderbrand, Klopfer, and Walker and Simo, as well as popular essays such as Calvin Tomkin's in *The New Yorker*, have greatly expanded professional awareness of his work and its significance in twentieth-century modernism.[4] Yet, most of these essays are limited in their treatment of Kiley's spatiality. On the one hand, they define it formally and geometrically in relationship to a few sources, mostly architectural, such as Frank Lloyd Wright and Mies van der Rohe. On the other hand, they note Kiley's reminiscences of his personal experiences walking through the New England rural landscape of meadows, orchards, and woodlots. More as a result of focused reading for my lectures than any primary research into Kiley's archive, I have to wonder about these narrowly-framed and separate accounts of space, as they preclude more nuanced interpretations of Kiley's design contributions that are alluded to in his comments at the 1982 symposium about movement through the space defined by trees, "I think of design in the landscape as being like a walk in nature."[5]

This essay will examine a few additional ways to consider space in Kiley's designed landscapes beyond the formal, geometric, and architectural. In doing so, I will describe other accounts of space that were well-known in mid-twentieth-century design literature, and reveal possible links between Kiley and theories of landscape modernism as well as architecture. I will do this in two sections, begin-ning with a discussion of formal and lived space in Kiley's work and within the discourse of modernism, followed by an analysis of the particular spatiality of plants and the role of planted form in one of Kiley's iconic projects, the Irwin and Xenia Miller garden in Columbus, Indiana, designed and constructed between 1955 and 1957. I will conclude with a contextual analysis of the Miller garden that reframes this inquiry within larger spatial scales, uncovering new meanings of the garden, and speculating about the pervasiveness of spatial preoccupations in Kiley's creative process.

/ TWO SPATIAL CONCEPTS: ABSTRACT, ENCLOSED, FORMAL SPACE, VERSUS LIVED, PERCEIVED, EMBODIED SPACE /

Use of the term *space* in design theory was rare before the twentieth century. While building walls and garden walls have always shaped voids within which human life occurred, it wasn't until the eighteenth century that designers began describing the experience of architecture and gardens volumetrically. [6] As Adrian Forty chronicles in *Words and Buildings*, the term *space* is introduced into architectural design theory in the late nineteenth and twentieth centuries through philosophy.[7] This spatial discourse has two main threads, one focused on enclosure of space as the essential task of design and the other asserting the human body's importance for the perception of space. The first thread is a formalist position and assumes space exists as a volume independent of human life or experience. Space definition could be room-like and fully enclosed, or free-plan, implied, and continuous. The second thread emphasizes the experiential aspects of architecture and designed landscapes, and connects space to character, mood, and the emotions. This conception of space is lived, embodied, and not an abstraction. Both these threads can be found in the lectures and writings of educators, theorists, and designers who would have been familiar to American architects and landscape architects like Kiley, who was educated at Harvard in the mid-1930s and practicing on the East Coast in the 1940s and 1950s. Curiously, most writings about Kiley reference only the former, and not the latter.

/ MODERNIST SPATIAL PRECURSORS AND PREOCCUPATIONS /

In the decade before Kiley started his studies at Harvard, popular professional magazines in both architecture and landscape architecture published articles that mentioned spatial preoccupations, structural innovations, and functionalism as key characteristics of modernist design. For instance, Frank Lloyd Wright's first published use of the term *space* occurred in 1928 when he defined "architecture as interior-space finding interior utilization and enclosure as its 'members'—as architecture."[8] Two years later, in one of the first articles published in the United States on modernist garden explorations in Europe, landscape architect Fletcher Steele praised the garden designer Gabriel Guevrekian who, "designs in three dimensions" and "thinks in terms of volume."[9] In 1936, Steele's essay on "Modern Garden Design" defined the modern garden designer as a person who "designs in volumes rather than surfaces."[10] Moreover, Steele, one of the few practitioners respected by Kiley and his classmates Garrett Eckbo and James Rose, asserted that a shift towards spatial thinking and making would allow landscape architects to move beyond the tired formal and informal debates that had permeated the profession since the Blomfield and Robinson debates of the 1890s. Steele, who wrote over two dozen articles on contemporary design and theory during the decade before Kiley started studying landscape architecture, should be acknowledged as introducing him and his classmates to spatial concepts, and for encouraging more exploration into the ways these concepts could be applied to designing landscapes.[11]

It did not take long for these concepts to surface in writings by Kiley, or about his work. In 1939, a year after Siegfried Gideon presented the Harvard University Charles Eliot Norton lectures that were eventually published as *Space, Time and Architecture: The Growth of a New Tradition*, a series of articles on landscape design was published in *Architectural Record*.[12] Co-written by Eckbo, Kiley, and Rose, they have been described as a three-part manifesto. The first article, "Landscape Design in the Urban Environment," referred to volume and space as the tool for integrating interiors and exteriors and for creating healthy urban environments. They wrote,

> The most urgent need is the establishment of a bio-
> logical relationship between outdoor and indoor
> volumes which will automatically control density.
> This implies the integration of indoors and outdoors,
> of living space, working space, play space, of whole
> social units whose size is determined by the accessi-
> bility of its parts… It is possible to integrate landscape
> again with building—on a newer and higher plane—
> and thus achieve that sense of being environed in
> great and pleasantly organized space which charac-
> terized the great landscapes of the past.[13]

Their conception of space is multivalent; it is formal, functional, and biological, affording "a skeleton of volumes which are perforated enough to permit air and sunlight for plant growth. Plants now replace the interior parti-tions, and divide space for outdoor use."[14] As Anita Berrizbeitia has written, a strong functional strain per-meates these essays. Space is not a cool, abstract medium, but a vessel for social life.[15] This is evident in Eckbo, Kiley, and Rose's conclusion of this essay, where they address the unique spatial properties of plants alone and in combination: "The technics are more complicated than in the Beaux-Arts patterns, but we thereby achieve volumes of organized space in which people live and play, rather than stand and look."[16]

So, some thirty years before Kiley designs the Miller garden, and almost twenty-five years before he writes another article in a design journal, there is a record of his interest in space as a medium, a mode of organization, a tool for balancing development and health, and a vessel for life.[17] We can trace a lineage to the writings of Fletcher Steele, who advocated for landscape architecture's modernism through a spatial lens.

/ DOMINANT NARRATIVE: FROM MIESIAN FREE PLAN TO MODERNIST LANDSCAPE SPACE /

So why do so many narratives connect Kiley to the free plan seen in architect Ludwig Mies van der Rohe's Barcelona Pavilion, and in de Stijl spatial concepts?[18] As most Kiley scholars over the last decade have recounted, Dan often spoke of the excitement he and his Harvard chums felt over the spatial organization of the 1929 German Pavilion designed by Mies van der Rohe for the Barcelona International Exhibition. While none of them visited the building during its short life on the western slope of Barcelona's urban mountain, Montjuïc, it was widely published and could have been known to them from any number of sources. They most likely knew the pavilion through the one plan and two black-and-white photographs included in *The International Style*, Henry-Russell Hitchcock and Philip Johnson's 1932 catalog of the Museum of Modern Art's influential exhibition. It is described as follows in the chapter entitled "A First

Principle: Architecture as Volume" through spatial vocabulary:

> In the Barcelona Pavilion the walls are screens but they do not define a fixed volume. The volume beneath the post-supported slab roof is in a sense bounded by imaginary planes. The walls are independent screens set up within this total volume, having each a separate existence and creating subordinate volumes. The design is unified by the slab roof on its regular supports, not by the usual continuous exterior screen wall.[19]

This building plan, one of the most abstract in the exhibition catalog, with no labels or readily identifiable interior mechanical spaces, could easily be re-imagined as a landscape of garden walls, hedges, and tree trunks defining exterior volumes. Why not imagine an analogous text, such as "The garden is unified by the tree canopy on its regular trunks, not by the usual continuous perimeter hedge wall"?

Granted, there is graphic evidence that Kiley's classmates appreciated Mies van der Rohe's plan. The German Pavilion plan showed up in Eckbo's graduate thesis project as a community center within a residential superblock.[20] He was leaving breadcrumbs for future historians, no doubt. Rose also included a plan by Mies van der Rohe in one of his *Pencil Points* articles, but it is not the German Pavilion in Barcelona. Rather is it his 1922 Brick Country House. Thin planes, orthogonally arranged to partially enclose space but not form bounded rooms, characterize both of Mies's plans. Instead these lines create continuity with ambiguity between inside and outside as the wall planes and ceiling planes do not align with one another. In his *Pencil Points* article, Rose juxtaposed the Mies plan with a black-and-white reproduction of a de Stijl painting by Theo von Doesburg called *Russian Dance*,[21] a pairing he borrowed from the Museum of Modern Art catalog *Cubism and Abstract Art*. This catalog, documenting a exhibition held while Eckbo, Rose, and Kiley were in graduate school, compared these two images, painting and building plan, on the same page using the same descriptive terms—"broken, asymmetrical, orthogonal character of the plan."[22] If a MOMA curator compared paintings and buildings using the same vocabulary, why not expand that set to include paintings, buildings, gardens, and landscapes?

So, while Kiley does not learn about formal or conceptual space from architectural writings alone, he does come to appreciate a particular type of spatial organization, the free plan, or de Stijl space, from painting and/or architecture. Most critics assert that it was only through the spatial explorations in architecture that landscape architecture was reinvigorated as a modernist enterprise.[23] This assessment is too narrowly framed, as it does not examine the written sources about landscape spatiality from the first two decades of the twentieth century that were surely known to Kiley and his classmates. I think the influences were more varied, and I discern that the innovations in Kiley's landscape spatiality manifest themselves in ways that were as much about the traditions of his discipline as they were about modernist architecture's spatial principles and free plans.

/ THEORIES FROM WITHIN: LANDSCAPE ARCHITECTURE'S SPATIAL TRADITIONS /

One key source for my argument is a 1918 article with the radical title "Space Composition" that appeared in *Landscape Architecture* magazine written by its editor, Charles Downing Lay; this article appeared ten years before Frank Lloyd Wright first used the term *space* in his writing.[24] Lay, the magazine's founder, was one of the first graduates of the landscape architecture program at Harvard. He was the son of a painter, and his article was replete with references to art critics, such as George Santayana, Adolf Hildebrand, and Bernard Berenson, as well as more expected references to figures in landscape architecture from Humphry Repton to Charles Eliot. Lay argued that space composition is the "first thing to look for in works of landscape architecture," for, as Berenson wrote about painting, "space composition is the bone and marrow of the art of landscape."[25] He discussed space as "the arrangement of objects with relationship to one another" and said space must be "circumscribed, measurable." Lay asserted that this spatial focus is inevitable for landscape architecture by invoking Santayana's *The Sense of Beauty* (1896): "Nature allows herself to be accurately conceived only in spatial terms."[26] Through these passages, Lay established the basis for Steele's writings a decade later in which he discerned innovation occurring when the landscape's medium is defined as ground, plants, water, and space, the space between elements and the space formed by them.[27]

But Lay was not a pure or narrow formalist. He situated his argument within both of the spatial theories I alluded to previously, the formal and lived, the abstract and embodied, the conceptual and perceptual. In fact, Lay reminds his readers that art evokes an "emotional response that comes from its spatial composition" and is "apprehended in the mind." In other words, space is embodied and perceived, it is lived and experienced. Lay was drawing on the writings of contemporary art critics, such as Adolf Hildebrand, when he asserted that all the arts share a common condition —that they are defined by the emotions they evoke, and it is space consciousness that prompts that response.[28]

Lay illustrated these concepts with several examples from the history of landscape architecture, such as a Boston park by Charles Eliot and the chateau gardens of André Le Nôtre, and in doing so demonstrated that space composition could be found in a range of types of landscapes, from the pastoral park to the geometric parterre and bosque.[29] This leap from paintings and sculpture, the subject of Hildebrand's writing, to architecture and landscapes is credible given sections in Hildebrand, such as "Vision and Motion" and "The Idea of Space and Its Visual Expression." Hildebrand located spatial apprehension in vision and the movement of the eye. For a landscape architect such as Lay and his audience, this kinesthetic visual experience would, of course, include not only the eye, but the body, moving in and through space.[30]

/ KILEY'S VOLUMETRIC AND KINESTHETIC SPATIAL IMAGININGS /

In Lay's article, published in one of only two American landscape architecture journals of the early twentieth century, I find resonances with Kiley's two often repeated stories about landscapes that inspired him, for both are full of spatial imaginings and charged with affect.[31]

I heard both stories in Charlottesville during the 1982 symposium, and they have been reprinted, in similar form, in almost every article and book on Kiley. The first story evokes the spatial experience of walking through a rural landscape of orchards, woodlots, and forests.

> I think of design in the landscape as being like a walk in nature. It's all there, really, instead of copying the end result of a natural process, which the landscape architecture profession has done, especially ever since the mid or even early eighteenth century. From then on, landscape architects were always copying something. But the walk in nature is exciting and original, a fresh experience where you are going through a deep wood, maybe a grove of beech trees, then you come into an open meadow and you walk up the hill and then you come into the sugar maples, or "sugar-bush," as they call it in Vermont, and you walk through that. You squeeze in between trunks, and it's always moving and changing spatially. It's dynamic. This is the thing that intrigued and excited me right from the beginning. What I have been trying to do in my work is create a man-made scene having those attributes or characteristics.[32]

These experiences, close to his Vermont home as an adult, recall his childhood memories of playing at his grandmother's farm in New Hampshire. Most accounts of this narrative do not integrate it into a discourse of modernist spatial theories and principles, despite the clear resonance between Kiley's descriptions of walking through the spatially overlapping, tree-trunk punctuated rhythms of the dynamic, ever-changing meadows and woodlots of vernacular rural landscapes and the spatial sequence through a de Stijl free plan. Rather, these "walks in the woods" remain a part of a biographical background that is not directly connected to Kiley's modernist spatial vocabulary.

The other story involved a second type of landscape that moved him—the vast bosques of trees in French public parks, such as the Tuileries, and royal gardens, such as Versailles, Sceaux, and Vaux-le-Vicomte. While known to Kiley through black-and-white lantern slides while he was a student, the geometric arrangements of gridded tree plantings on a large scale were not truly apprehended by him until the end of World War II. With considerable insight, Peter Walker and Melanie Simo summarize their interviews with Kiley about this revelation in their book, *Invisible Gardens*:

> Nothing had prepared him, then, for the experience of walking along poplar—or sycamore—shaded paths of fine, yielding gravel and gazing upon serene canals and shafts of space extended into infinity...once Kiley had experienced the actual space, the scale, and the sensuous details of Le Nôtre's great work, the whole French design tradition and other works of the past became accessible and exciting to him.[33]

Five years before his death, Kiley published a book with Jane Amidon in which he connects those experiences walking in French gardens and parks to those perambulating around his home in Charlotte, Vermont:

> I suddenly saw that lines, allées and orchards / bosques of trees, tapis verts and clipped hedges, canals, pools and fountains could be tools to build landscapes of clarity and infinity, just like a walk in the woods. I did not see then, and to this day do not see, a problem with using classic elements in modern compositions,

*for this is not about style of decoration but about
articulation of space. The thing that is modern is
space.*[34]

Here we sense the power of spatial thinking and making to
connect conceptual organization and perceptual experience.
We realize that Kiley was not primarily interested in
Wright or Mies or de Stijl, but in constructing dynamic,
kinesthetic spatial experiences using planted forms. Rows,
allées, orchards, and bosques were forms that were means
to an end. As Kiley wrote in the 1960s, "Landscape design,
as in building design, is the organization of space to satisfy
certain human functions," and "I am delighted and amazed
when I set a little bit of geometry in space and see it
develop and grow and seek infinite relationships outward
to the universe or rather with the universe."[35] For Kiley,
by the mid 1940s, the lived, kinetic space of changing
landscape held more interest than the two-dimensional
visual landscape or the patterned landscape that he ascribed
to nineteenth-century and early-twentieth-century Beaux-
Arts designers.

In this regard, Kiley was not alone. Design critics such as
Erno Goldfinger in "The Sensation of Space" in *Architectural
Review* or László Moholy-Nagy writing of "flowing fields
of force" in *The New Vision* were describing the space of
architecture as formal and lived, abstract and experienced.[36]
So when Kiley told my friend Anne that I should talk
about his work in "3 dimensions," and to be sure to assign
Italian architectural historian and theorist Bruno Zevi's
book, it should not have been surprising. In *Architecture
as Space*, Zevi describes architecture happening when
"man moving about within the building, studying it from
successive points of view, himself creates, so to speak, the
fourth dimension, giving the space an integrated reality."
He adds, "That space—void—should be the protagonist
of architecture is after all natural. Architecture is not
art alone, it is not merely a reflection of the conditions
of life or a portrait of systems of living. Architecture is
environment, the stage on which our lives unfold."[37]

/ NEW COLLABORATORS: FROM INTERIOR SPACE TO SPATIALLY INTEGRATED HOUSE+GARDEN /

By the time that Kiley received the commission he described
as the best work of his career, the Irwin and Xenia
Miller garden in Columbus, Indiana, it was commonplace
for these "architectural ideas" to have stretched to include
the landscape. In the early 1940s, Erno Goldfinger and
Eliel Saarinen, the father of Eero, the Miller's architect,
were writing about the need for intentionally-shaped space
outside of architecture's interior volumes.[38] Saarinen's
book *The City: Its Growth, Its Decay, Its Future* criticized
early-twentieth-century modern architecture for ignoring
the space outside of and between buildings, for limiting
their "art of space" to interior volumes.[39] So when
Christopher Tunnard's 1938 *Gardens in the Modern
Landscape* was reprinted after World War II, it is not
surprising that a new essay on space and the modern
garden was added, written by architect Joseph Hudnut,
the Dean of the Harvard Graduate School of Design
(GSD) who hired Tunnard and Walter Gropius in the
1930s.[40] Tunnard was received with great enthusiasm by
students and recent alums, such as Kiley, when he taught
at the GSD from 1939–43. It is very likely that Kiley read
this second edition and was familiar with this passage:

*I am inclined to believe that this aesthetic is more
clearly exhibited in the new quality of space and in*

*the new command of space: a space free as in no
other architecture from the tyranny of structure…
Gardens like houses, are built of space. Gardens are
fragments of space set aside by the planes of terraces
and walls and disciplined foliage. Until now we have
defined too nicely the difference between that space
which is roofed and within the house and that which is
left outside and around the house… The new vision has
dissolved the ancient boundary between architecture
and landscape architecture. The garden flows into and
over the house: through the loggias and courts and
wide areas of clear glass, and over roofs and sun-rooms
and canopied terraces. The house reaches out into
the garden with walls and terraced enclosures that
continue its rhythms and share its grace. The concordant
factor is the new quality of space.*[41]

We should consider the appearance of a house and garden
as spatially integrated as the Miller garden in relationship
to changing conceptions of space on the part of architects,
and not only on Kiley's newfound appreciation of space.
For twenty years, he and his peers had been designing
spatially. In the 1950s, Kiley finally found some architects
interested in the spatiality of "landscape." As Zevi wrote,
the experience of space "has its extension in the city, in
the streets, squares, alleys and parks, in the playgrounds
and in the gardens, wherever man has defined and limited
a void and so has created an enclosed space."[42] There were
many spatial alternatives to the paradigm of a discrete
object building—an ideal white box—set in an amorphous
pastoral open space masquerading as nature. One of those
alternatives—a spatially integrated interior and exterior—
promised new kinds of functional, biophysical, and kinesthetic joints between buildings and gardens, requiring
landscape architects to think critically about plants as
a spatial medium as well as from a horticultural and
ecological perspective.

/ THE SPATIALITY OF LANDSCAPE: PLANTED FORM AND THE GARDEN /

How do plants define space? Landscape space is quali-
tatively different from architectural space even when the
same spatial principles are deployed. Landscape is not
"climate controlled" as it does not have a weather-tight
enclosure of walls, windows, and roof. Exterior spaces are
dependent on ceilings and floors—the horizontal planes
above and below—for their enclosure even more than
walls or vertical planes. By ceiling, I am referring to a
tree canopy's lower surface defined by a tree's branches
and leaves. The space between that ceiling and the ground
is a palpable space, a shady place sheltered from the sun
and separated from the sky. The character of this space is
dependent on many variables, from the shape and texture
of the leaf and its darkness of tone to the size and shape of
the canopy, the season of the year, the scent of the tree's
flowers, the shape of its fruit and nuts, and even the way
its leaves transmit backlit rays of the sun at day's end.
This is not to say there are no walls in the landscape, of
course. Stone walls, clipped hedges, loose shrub masses,
and vine scrims separate and join spaces to one another.
The trunks of trees, if spaced close enough together, are
perceived as a perforated wall, as if a window existed
between each tree column. Horizontal surfaces, vertical
surfaces, and masses collectively contribute to a landscape's
spatial enclosure and extension, as well as to the experience
of *space sensation* in that landscape [figure 4–1].

Kiley and his peers, Eckbo and Rose, addressed the specific role that plants play in the delineation of space in their late 1930s articles. In doing so, they were operating within what we have come to know, through art critic Clement Greenberg, as modernist norms wherein artists sought to exploit the specific properties and logic of their medium. While Rose was the most systematic in creating a taxonomy of planted form in his book *Creative Gardens* [figure 4–2] and through his charts in Margaret O. Goldsmith's *Designs for Outdoor Living*, the three of them are on record in 1939 about the key role plants would play in reshaping the urban environment: "Plants now replace the interior partitions, and divide space for outdoor use."[43] Kiley's designed landscape at the Miller garden is heralded as an icon of mid-twentieth-century modernist space created by planted form, but it is indebted to the writing and making of Eckbo and Rose in the 1930s and 1940s. Collectively, these writings, building on those of Charles Downing Lay and Fletcher Steele, constitute a declaration of first principles for designing modernist spatial landscapes, underscoring the unique attributes of their medium and discipline.

Eckbo's 1941 article, "Outdoors and In: Gardens as Living Space," calls for gardens to be more than places to grow plants; they should be outdoor spaces for living shaped by walls, loose untrimmed hedges, and a "transparent plane of a row of tree trunks or columns."[44] The term transparent has a double reading. It refers to the language of modern art and architecture, implying a connection with the transparency of building walls made of large sheets of glass or the overlap of transparent forms in abstract art. But transparent also refers to an actual

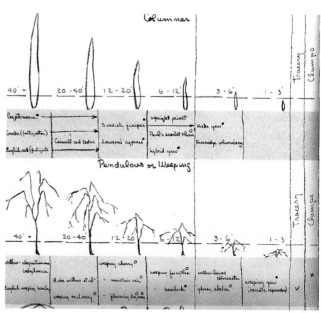

condition of planted form. Even when in leaf, a tree is not a solid mass.

A tree is not simply green *poché*, to use the Beaux-Arts terminology for the rendering of the mass of a thick wall. It can provide varying densities of enclosure, from a wall and a screen to a scrim and a veil. Depending on the time of year, a bosque of trees or row of shrubs possesses varying degrees of mass and enclosure, as its canopy changes from translucent in early spring to opaque in summer to transparent in winter. As a source for inspiration and to illustrate this concept, Eckbo returned to the rural landscape that was the subject of the Eckbo, Kiley, and Rose article a few years before, "Landscape Design in the Rural Environment." In a passage printed on the same page as a Kiley sketch for a Princeton garden, Eckbo wrote:

> And there we do find innumerable definite three-dimensional space forms produced with both structural and natural materials: rectangular or polygonal fields cut from solid natural wildwoods; straight lines of untrimmed hedges and mixed hedgerows, and of fences and old stone walls, grown up with natural plants; free-standing clumps of trees forming natural pavilions; intersecting planes of these lines of trees and hedges and walls forming a fragmentary organization of space. It is seldom enclosed; always there is a suggestion of its continuity, something to follow, the stimulating impossibility of seeing all of the space at once.[45]

I am not sure who is channeling whom here, Eckbo to Kiley or Kiley to Eckbo, but this passage written in 1941 captures the same experience that Kiley described as "his walk through the woods." Regardless of authorship, collectively they assign plants configured with intention —planted form—an experiential and structural role. Plants delineate an area and give it boundaries; they shape space, and are spatial. Given the degree of transparency or opacity of a plant, they also layer upon one another, and slip in front and behind one another as a person moves through and lives within the spaces they define.

Kiley's other classmate, James Rose, wrote six articles in *Pencil Points* illustrated with models he made of hypothetical gardens that demonstrate spatial thinking and making. His cutting and folding of paper, loofah, and other found objects—clearly inspired by the Kurt Schwitters ready-made collages and Naum Gabo constructions he publishes alongside them—suggest how written descriptions of plants could lead to new ways of construing and imagining designed landscapes: "The constructivists probably have the most to offer landscape design because their work deals with space relations in volume. The sense of transparency, and of visibility broken by a succession of planes, as found in their constructions, if translated in terms of outdoor material, would be an approach sufficient to free us from the limitation imposed by the axial system."[46] [figure 4–3] Further, "The intrinsic beauty and meaning of a landscape design comes from the organic relationship between materials and the division of space in volume to express and to satisfy the use for which it is intended."[47] Rose's three-dimensional models, and passages such as these, are calls for thinking about plants as a spatial medium and creating analytical tools for categorizing them according to their space-making capacities and potentials. Rose takes this on in the form of illustrated plant form charts published in at least two sources.[48] Kiley cites one of these sources, Goldsmith's *Designs for*

/ **4–1** / *opposite left*
DAN KILEY, MILLER GARDEN, COLUMBUS, INDIANA, 1955.
SPACE BETWEEN CANOPY AND GROUND.
/ WILLIAM MORRISH /

/ **4–2** / *opposite right*
JAMES ROSE, PLANT FORM CHARTS, 1958.
/ *CREATIVE GARDENS*, 1958, COURTESY THE JAMES ROSE FOUNDATION /

Outdoor Living, as an influence during the period before he designed the Miller garden.[49]

From this abbreviated account of the theoretical design discourse on space in early to mid-twentieth-century American landscape architecture publications—professional journals, not arcane sources—it is apparent that by the early 1950s modernist architecture is conceived in relationship to spatially defined landscapes and cities; that it is not solely construed as free-standing buildings with highly articulated interior spatial volumes in some untouched natural environment, a view typical of many earlier modernist architects; that modernist landscape architecture is presumed to be spatially innovative as well as functionally responsible; and that one vehicle for exploring the modernist spatial potentials of landscape was to arrange plants according to their own volumetric qualities and in combination with the qualities of others.[50]

/ NEW DIRECTIONS FOR KILEY RESEARCH: PLANTED FORM AND SPATIALITY, SPATIAL SEQUENCES, AND SITUATED SPACE /

I believe there is still much to be gained from situating Kiley's work and words within this theoretical discourse, despite all his protestations that theory didn't matter. (As my students hear me say each year at the start of my Theories of Modern Landscape Architecture course, there is no such thing as a designer without a theoretical position. There are only those who admit their theoretical position and those who are so dogmatic they cannot appreciate there is any other position but their own, or who claim to base their work on some kind of mysterious "intuition" that is not subject to analysis.) By expanding the spatial

references from one to many, Kiley's work is not diminished, but enriched. He can be understood as existing within, and participating in, a discourse that was as much about continuities as ruptures, and as much about the discipline of landscape architecture as architecture.

What, if anything, can this expanded context contribute to our interpretation of Dan Kiley's body of work, or to the methods we deploy when studying his gardens and designed landscapes? If we are to examine and evaluate his projects in relationship to his own words, we must move beyond analyzing his gardens through the exclusive language of de Stijl or Miesian spatial theories. In the second half of this essay, I will suggest several lenses for future scholarship in this regard:

1. Planted form. A more nuanced look at the plant species in Kiley's landscapes, especially their qualities and characteristics, as they impact spatial structure, enclosure, and densities.

2. Spatial sequences. Careful on-site documentation and analysis, as well as digital reconstruction, of the ways Kiley's projects approximate his "walk through the woods," followed by use of more precise and expansive vocabulary for describing the spatial principles within his work.

3. Contextual analysis. An expanded assessment of the sites and cities where Kiley's projects are located to ascertain how the garden's spatial structure and experience is impacted by its surrounding spatial fields and matrices of city, suburb, and countryside.

/4-3/ *left*
**JAMES ROSE,
HYPOTHETICAL GARDEN
MODEL.**
GARDEN GROUND FORMS
AND SPACE, COMPARED
TO ARTWORK BY
GEORGES BRAQUE AND
KURT SCHWITTERS.
/ *PENCIL POINTS,* OCTOBER
1938, COURTESY THE JAMES
ROSE FOUNDATION /

/4-4/ *opposite left*
**MILLER GARDEN,
COLUMBUS, INDIANA.
HORSE-CHESTNUT ALLÉE.**
/ WILLIAM MORRISH /

/4-5/ *opposite right*
**MILLER GARDEN.
FIGURE-GROUND DIAGRAM.**
/ ELIZABETH MEYER AND
SHANTI LEVY /

I will apply these lenses to one of Kiley's best known and analyzed gardens, the Miller garden, to demonstrate the efficacy of these arenas for studying Kiley's other gardens and designed landscapes.

/ PLANTED FORM AND THE SPACES OF THE MILLER GARDEN /

What may be learned by looking more closely at the Miller garden's planted form? [figure 4–4] As the diagrams that accompany this essay demonstrate, the spatial organization and character of the Miller garden are more complex than a pure figure-ground drawing of it would suggest [figure 4–5].[51] Until one adds the canopy as an in-between condition in a figure-ground, the spatial enclosure of plants is reduced, by graphics, to the vertical condition of hedges and tree trunks [figure 4–6]. Once the canopy is added the garden is understood less in terms of geometries and axes, and more in terms of densities of spatial enclosure; it is understood less in terms of vertical planes or objects and more in terms of ceilings and floors [figure 4–7]. This hybrid figure-ground allows the space between figure and ground to emerge, a condition I have described as "articulated space" in my lecture course and earlier writings. This term resonates with Rose's fascination with Gabo's space-sculpture, and it translates Colin Rowe's writing on architectural transparency into the language of landscape.[52]

In this modified figure-ground, the house is still differentiated by the density of its canopy (sliced through by its linear systems of skylights), but it is less a center of influence and more part of a gradient of spaces defined between ceiling and floor with varying shade/light qualities.

Especially revealing is a comparison of the traditional figure-ground [see figure 4–5] with a drawing of just the horizontal planes of enclosure—floor + ceiling, or ground + canopy [see figure 4-7]. In this ceiling and floor diagram, one senses the contrast between adjacent and sequential spaces: the densely planted *Aesculus* species horse chestnut allée that lines the entrance driveway and the open parking court [figure 4–8; see also figure 4-4]; the juxtaposition and balance between the verticality of the *Quercus alba*, white oak, bosque and the low horizontality of the adjacent house; the contrast between the monumentality of the mature white oak bosque near the car court and the more intimate scale of the plan grid and tree canopy in the *Malus* species apple bosques that enclose the children's play areas south of the house [figure 4–9]. The cross-sections through these spaces suggest the different spatial densities created by the various plant species and spacings [figure 4–10]. They also demonstrate that the traditional figure-ground plan [see figure 4–5] emphasizes the role of the house as center and generator of geometries. The sections and canopy plans reveal an alternative conception of the garden's center that is not dependent on the house. These drawings reveal a diptych at the center of the plan created by the spatial tension between two elements—the low house and the tall oak bosque, between a horizontal line and a vertical mass.

Are there additional lessons to be gleaned from a more nuanced reading of the spatiality of plants in this garden? When those smooth grey-tones are substituted with varying textures representing some of the quality of the shade cast by the different species of trees [figure 4–11], then the distinctions between the horse chestnut and *Gleditsia*

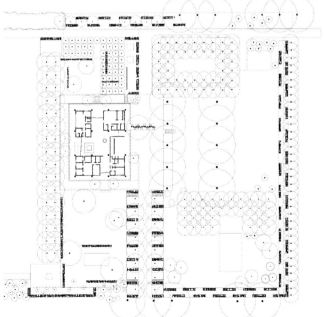

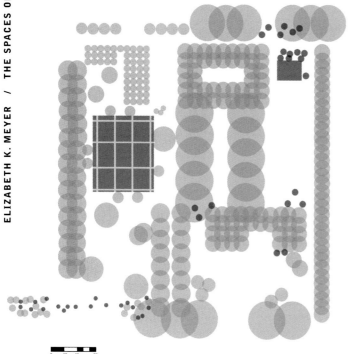

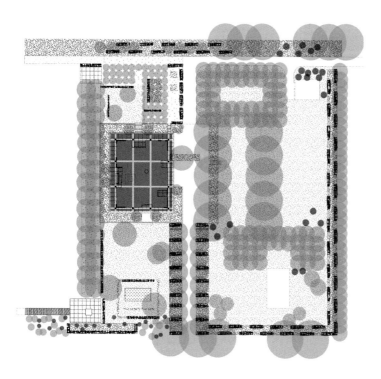

triacanthos, honey-locust, allées become more apparent [figure 4–12]. The former has been discussed by many critics, including Bleam, Olin, Hilderbrand, and Johnson, as innovative for its orientation—parallel with the western facade of the house like a huge portico or sun-visor. When seen in relationship to the entrance allée, the honey-locust performs in new ways. Its small, compound leaves filter the bright western summer light, and then intensify the setting sun's color in autumn when the light's intensity diminishes. The large, palmately compound leaves of the horse chestnut do the opposite, reinforcing the threshold by exaggerating the shade. One drives through them towards the north, so the sunny patch of the parking courtyard ahead gleams under the dense, dark green canopy—what Kiley called a "tight, dark green tunnel" [figure 4-8].[53] Each plant is understood and experienced in relationship to its adjacent condition and solar orientation. By thinking about plant particularities and properties, new questions emerge. Was the adults' garden (*Cercis canadensis* redbud bosque) located to the north to be away from the street? Or perhaps to be sheltered from the winter winds that come from the south? Did this allow the redbuds to bloom later than in other parts of town where they were not sheltered, thus extending springtime? Or was the tree chosen for the adults' garden because the leaves are heart-shaped?

Considering species as well as spacing allows us to imagine the perceptual aspects of the Miller garden's spaces; a focus on specific plants suggests other spatialities, and perhaps the memories associated with them. For instance, the 15-feet-on-center apple tree bosques were planted with trees from the Miller's nearby farm, so Mrs. Miller could use their fruits in apple pies. They were practical

/ 4-6 /
MILLER GARDEN,
COLUMBUS, INDIANA.
CANOPY DIAGRAM.
/ ELIZABETH MEYER AND
SHANTI LEVY /
/ 4-7 /
MILLER GARDEN.
CANOPY-GROUND
TEXTURE DIAGRAM.
/ ELIZABETH MEYER AND
SHANTI LEVY /

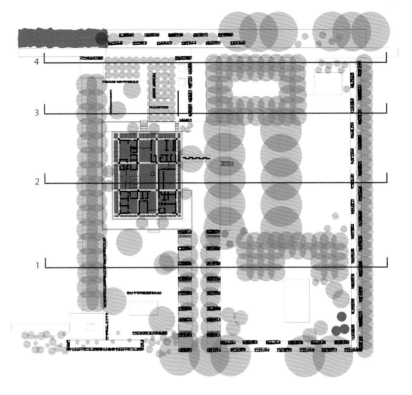

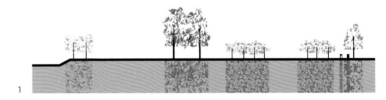

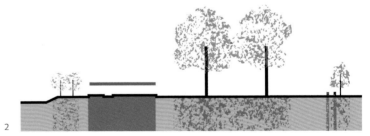

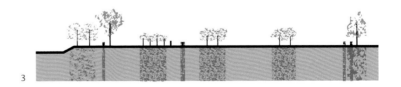

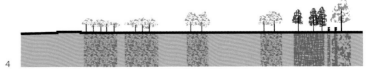

/ **4-8** / *left above*
MILLER GARDEN.
HORSE CHESTNUT ALLÉE.
/ WILLIAM MORRISH /
/ **4-9** / *left below*
MILLER GARDEN.
APPLE BOSQUE ACROSS
MEADOW.
/ WILLIAM MORRISH /
/**4-10**/ *right*
MILLER GARDEN.
SITE PLAN AND SECTIONS.
/ ELIZABETH MEYER AND
SHANTI LEVY /

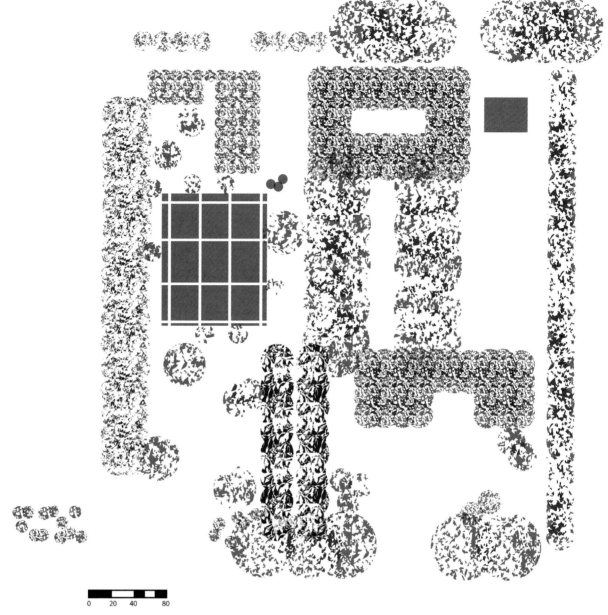

/ 4–11 /
MILLER GARDEN,
COLUMBUS, INDIANA, 1955.
CANOPY TEXTURE DIAGRAM
(DENSITY OF SHADE).
/ ELIZABETH MEYER AND
SHANTI LEVY /
/ 4–12 /
MILLER GARDEN.
HONEY-LOCUST ALLÉE,
LOOKING NORTH.
/ WILLIAM MORRISH /

0   20   40   80

and functional, yes. But they also evoked memories for the family of other beloved spaces—of the rural agrarian landscape just beyond this suburbanizing edge of Columbus, as well the vernacular landscape whose industrial agriculture was powered by the Cummins' engines that fueled the family's wealth. The horse chestnuts of the entry drive allée were not native to Indiana, but their references would have resonated with Kiley, if not with the Millers. This species characterized the Tuileries, in Paris, one of the Le Nôtre gardens that Kiley spoke of so enthusiastically when he recounted experiencing the powerful geometries and memorable spaces of seventeenth-century French gardens.

While much attention has been given to plant species that are grouped in monocultures to form lines and volumes in Kiley's landscapes, in his planting plan for the Miller garden he clearly considered plants as sculptural objects with textural qualities. Examples of this include several plants near the house. Kiley planted a *Fagus sylvatica 'pendula'*, weeping beech, along the translucent screen defining the north wall of the car court, a dramatic multi-stemmed form that was carefully and asymmetrically placed opposite the terminus of the entrance drive [figure 4–13]. He selected deciduous saucer magnolias, *Magnolia x soulangiana*, for the areas just outside the north and south entrances to the adults' and childrens' wings of the house [figure 4–14]. These, of course, produce large, pink blossoms —like an old-fashioned Easter bonnet—early in the spring. I am fascinated by the decision to plant them on both sides of the house, as I suspect the magnolias on the north would bloom several days, if not a week, after those on the south thus extending the species bloom and, by implication, extending spring as well. Both magnolias and weeping

/ **4-13** /
MILLER GARDEN.
WEEPING BEECH IN
THE CAR COURT.
/ WILLIAM MORRISH /

beech are multi-stemmed, broad trees that not only counter the horizontal mass of the building, but create small
enclosures between the exterior wall of the house and its
ceiling and terrace floor.

Two other trees with smooth bark and striking branching
structure like the magnolia and beech punctuate the spaces
near the house. Between the house and the adults' garden
redbud bosque, Kiley planted two *Cladastris lutea*, yellow-
wood, a species often confused with a beech because of
its bark and leaf shape, until its delicate, pendulous white
flowers bloom in the spring. In the southwest quadrant of
the garden, near the pool, he planted two *Fagus grandifolia*,
American beech, that hold their light brown leaves long
into winter. Thus, the beech trees would become even
more object-like in those months, their canopy of light
brown leaves rustling in the prevailing winter winds that
come from the south. In each case, the trees are within
a large enclosure, and not aligned with any of the adjacent
allées, rows, or bosques. So, again, the object quality of each
tree is reinforced by the spatial arrangement of the garden.
They function like the Kolbe statue in the Barcelona
Pavilion, or a shade tree in a cow pasture near a woodlot:
one solitary specimen standing out from its surroundings,
orienting and gathering bodies around it.

At some distance from the house, and placed near the
children's play court in the southeast corner of the site,
are trees with distinctive characteristics that would
make an outdoor room, well, more playful: *Oxydendron
arboreum,* sourwood, a native American tree not indigenous
to Indiana, with fragrant white flowers in July, scarlet
autumn leaves, and long tan capsules in the autumn;

Diospyros virginia, persimmon, an Indiana native with apricot leaves and fleshy yellow-orange fruits in the autumn that are great for eating—and throwing; *Syringa japonica*, Japanese lilac, a small tree with white blossoms in early summer; and *Koelreuteria paniculata*, golden raintree, a tree from China that is dripping with pale yellow pendulous flowers in mid-summer that are followed by large, light-green seed pods [figure 4–15]. There are few plants, especially trees, with prominent summer interest, so this concentration of such trees is significant, and underscored by plant expert Michael Dirr's account of the golden raintree, "Very lovely to look upon and lay under on a hot July day."[54] During the summer and early fall, these trees would shift the focus from the spatial enclosure of the northern apple bosque and the *Thuja* cultivar arborvitae hedge on the other three sides to the small groupings of the species mentioned above—sourwood, persimmon, Japanese lilac, and golden raintree. From June through November, one or more of these tree groupings would provide sights, scents, textures, and tastes for children playing in the garden. The distinct character and qualities of these trees provide a different kind of spatial density, and experiential note, that is lost when not looking closely at planted form, one key component of the landscape medium.

A composite diagram of vertical and horizontal enclosing elements—of canopies, floor, and walls—provides an even more complex, and landscape specific, spatial reading of the garden [figure 4–16]. The garden is enclosed by a perforated wall on three sides, but is open to the west. This first move defines the boundary of the garden through a technique common in the long history of gardens. This staggered hedge has nothing to do with de Stijl or Miesian

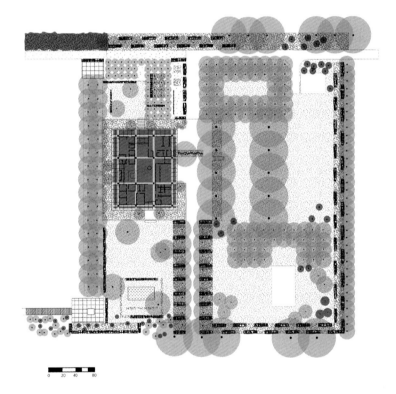

/ **4–14** / *opposite left*
MILLER GARDEN,
COLUMBUS, INDIANA, 1955.
SAUCER MAGNOLIA FLANK-
ING THE ENTRANCE TO THE
CHILDREN'S WING.
/ WILLIAM MORRISH /

/ **4–15** / *opposite right*
MILLER GARDEN.
GOLDEN RAINTREE AND
PERSIMMON IN THE
CHILDREN'S PLAY COURT
AREA.
/ WILLIAM MORRISH /

/ **4–16** /
MILLER GARDEN.
COMPOSITE DIAGRAM
OF FIGURE-GROUND AND
CANOPY-GROUND TEXTURE.
/ ELIZABETH MEYER AND
SHANTI LEVY /

space and everything to do with differentiating a garden from other types of designed landscapes [figure 4–17]. It is in this sense that John Dixon Hunt writes, "The garden will thus be distinguished in various ways from the adjacent territories in which it is set. Either it will have some precise boundary, or it will be set apart by the greater extent, scope and variety of its design and internal organization; more usually both will serve to designate its space and its actual or implied enclosure."[55] The perimeter hedge forms three sides of the garden, and makes an emphatic corner towards the city street; it does not radiate outwards, pinwheel-like, as do so many de Stijl free plans. It is defining an interior realm more than gesturing to the periphery.

This enclosing gesture wraps around a series of spatial figures—a house, a courtyard, three bosques, and a pool enclosure. Each figure is orthogonal and fits within an irregularly dimensioned grid. But none of the planted figures is centered on the center of the house or any of its columns. Each garden space is slightly shifted and at times de Stijl in its asymmetrical organization and varied openness (such as the adults' garden), as if we could still see the traces of Kiley seeking the direct dimension and location for each use. It is as if the de Stijl, Miesian, or Wrightian free plan is contained within an enclosed garden room, and the result is a hybrid spatial type, not simply the application of architectural spatial ideas to the landscape.

The varied gray tones of figure 4–11, singularly and through their overlap, imply densities of light and shadow within the garden. They offer additional clues about the place-making qualities of the garden, as space is created as much

/ 4–17 /
MILLER GARDEN,
COLUMBUS, INDIANA, 1955.
STAGGERED PERIMETER
HEDGE.
/ WILLIAM MORRISH /
/ 4–18 /
MILLER GARDEN.
HONEY-LOCUST ALLÉE.
SPACE CREATED BY
SATURATED COLOR, LIGHT,
AND SHADOW.
/ WILLIAM MORRISH /

/ 4–19 / opposite left
MILLER GARDEN.
ENTRANCE ALLÉE AND
LAWN.
SPACE CREATED BY
SATURATED COLOR, LIGHT,
AND SHADOW.
/ WILLIAM MORRISH /
/ 4–20 / opposite right
MILLER GARDEN.
GARDEN PLINTH AND
SIX-ACRE MEADOW.
/ WILLIAM MORRISH /

by different degrees of light and shade—and their associated ambient temperature and humidity—as enclosure [figures 4–18, 4–19]. Floating across the flat four-acre garden plinth and the lower, six-acre meadow and riparian forest, shadow creates planes of saturated color—more green, more golden, depending on the time of year [figure 4–20]—akin to the pools of light and color floating across the canvas of the one-meter by two-meter Monet painting, *Le bassin aux nympheas* (*Water Lily Pond*, 1919), that hung inside the house and recently sold at auction at Christie's in London.

/ SEQUENTIAL EXPERIENCE IN THE GARDEN /

I have been arguing that Kiley's landscape spaces were formal, geometrically precise, volumetric, and specific to the landscape medium. His gardens were imagined as volumes shaped by plants in different configurations—specimen, row, allée, bosque, grove—and of different characteristics—sizes, shapes, colors, and textures with an array of multi-sensory qualities. But I have also suggested that his recorded and public descriptions of landscape spaces were simultaneously embodied, experienced, perceptual, and kinesthetic. They evoked the mood and character of a place, how it made one feel as one moved through it. Here, my analysis is handicapped. For, while I have visited a dozen of Kiley's designed landscapes, I have not seen the Miller garden, except from North Washington Street to the east, and Riverside Drive to the south. Today, while the dense, shadowy mass of staggered hedges visible from the city street is fixed in my imagination, I know the Miller garden like most, through photographs and drawings. In addition to the excellent, informative Felice Frankel, Ezra Stoller, and Alan Ward photographs that have been published elsewhere, for five years I have been studying a

series of photographs taken by Catherine Brown and William Morrish in 1994 when they attended a Pritzker Prize dinner in the garden.[56] From the ideas sparked by my study of word, drawing, and image, I offer a few provisional observations of the spatial experience of the Miller garden that I believe could form the basis of future research by others.

1. *Spatial sequences.* I hope some scholar will interview the Miller children who grew up in this house and garden to ask them about how they lived and played in it, what times of day and season they used different areas, and for what purposes. By mapping these activities, their rhythms, routes, and memories, the garden's life after Kiley, what John Dixon Hunt has called its "afterlife," could be compared to Kiley's varied accounts of landscape experience.[57] Did the children play in the meadow, the car court, under the roof overhang, or mostly in the half-acre play garden located in the southeast quadrant? Did the children move back and forth from their play court to the pool and meadow along the staggered hedge and allée of maples that line the southern edge of the property? Did the family take after dinner walks along that allée to the river? What parts of the house and garden were for guests to experience? Was the adults' garden used by anyone else? These routines, and others only the family would know, are key to understanding the social space of the garden and remain to be explored.

Here, I do want to offer some observations about one spatial sequence that is apparent from the plan and that won't benefit from the social space analysis I call for above. It begins on the driveway leading from Riverside Drive into the car court, moves inside into the public rooms

of the house, and then exits onto the terrace and into either the north or south garden, the northwest and southwest quadrants respectively. Along these two sequences there is an alternating rhythmic sequence of moving from spaces defined by floors and ceilings, canopies and floors, to those open to the sky.

180-foot-long *shady* horse chestnut allée drive (20-by-32 feet on center)
60-by-100-foot *sunny* car court with *specimen* weeping beech
shady interior hall and living room
60-by-60-foot-square *sunny* lawn with *specimen* yellow-wood trees
shady redbud grove (10-by-10 feet on center)

180-foot-long *shady* horse chestnut allée drive (20-by-32 feet on center)
60-by-100-foot *sunny* car court with *specimen* weeping beech
shady interior hall and living room
180-by-120-foot *sunny* lawn with *specimen* beech and magnolias, and swimming enclosure
shady honey-locust allée (12-by-24 feet on center)

This staccato rhythm of spaces structures the sequence and differentiates spaces by degrees of shade and light as well as enclosure. The shady rooms have low ceilings or canopies that are their primary enclosing surfaces. This creates analogies between exteriors and interiors, and explains the use of the sunny lawns as a lobby or threshold between space with ceiling (house) and space with ceiling (bosque). This analysis of the spatial rhythms also affords us insights to the deployment of the "trees as sculptural objects" that I mentioned previously. These trees are beacons to the outdoors, complex in branching habit, and texturally interesting in their extreme smoothness of bark. They occupy these sunny lawn rooms that the interiors open into, and are the few places where plants in the Miller garden read as objects or figures instead of walls or ceilings. This figuration is apprehended through movement and is fleeting as it depends on the apprehension of enclosure and sequence, before and after.

2. *House as garden wall or courtyard loggia*. The house, while substantial in size, almost 8,000 square feet, seems to function as much as a garden wall within a series of spatial sequences as a destination. Partially, this is the result of how one moves towards the house obliquely or off center. It is also the result of the house being low and without much façade articulation. In fact, I have begun to think about the house with its wide perimeter overhanging roof and terrace as an "inside out" courtyard house. Each of the facades of the house forms a loggia edge to an outdoor room—car court, two lawn panels, and a meadow. The other sides of this turned inside out loggia are made with plants—hedges, tree trunks, and canopies [figure 4–21].

3. *Ceiling and floor*. Kiley's spaces are defined as much by ceilings and floors—canopies and ground—as they are by vertical surfaces such as hedges or tree trunks. Photographs of the garden depict the significance of the canopy as a definer of space, creator of shade, and modifier of microclimate. When a canopy plan of the garden is paired with a series of cross sections [see figures 4-6 and

4-10], one begins to understand why James Rose wrote, "I have often thought that most of the garden design problems would be solved if we started with a sky plan instead of a ground plan. The sky is really the ceiling of the garden."[58] This set of drawings is, for me, a shorthand, a placeholder, for all that could still be imagined and conjectured about the Miller garden's spatial order and experience. I hope someone with access to the garden, and the clients, takes this on soon.[59]

/ SITUATED SPACE, SCALING SPACE: FIRST, SECOND, AND THIRD NATURE IN THE MILLER GARDEN /

> Since most people now accept that the Utopia envisioned by modern architects was a miserable flop, the wonderful Daniel Urban Kiley show at the Urban Center may cause some visitors to rub their eyes in disbelief. What is this if not Utopia, this dappled, sunlit world of trees, lawns, fountains and flowers? Isn't this the garden city modern architects promised to cultivate along with their crisp Machine Age buildings? —Herbert Muschamp.[60]

It is not uncommon to hear Kiley's garden and landscape spaces described as utopian, as the marks of high modernism's stripped-down formalism, detached and cool formalism, devoid of contextual references and any rootedness in place. Accounts of Kiley's spatial references as de Stijl free plan play into and reinforce the reading of his work as cool, abstract, and detached high modernism. I find Kiley's gardens remarkable because they are about those issues and more. For, as his varied writings and musings about the experience of "walking in the woods," or

of seeing the American rural landscape from an airplane, or being at his grandparents' farm in New Hampshire demonstrate, Kiley thought of first and second nature, the wild or forest and the vernacular, rural landscape, as a referent when creating third nature, a garden or designed landscape.[61] His design language was multivalent, drawing on the vocabulary of abstraction and spatial theory, exploring the particularities of the landscape medium—especially plants and their arrangement—and recognizing the landscape architect's canvas—the immediate ground as well as the territory of the larger urban-suburban context.

I believe that the specific geographic situation of the Miller's property imbues this project of Kiley's with a richer spatial reading than many of his other projects [figure 4–22]. In the mid-1950s, this parcel was located on the northwestern periphery of the city. It sits at the seam between three spatial fields: a slightly irregular urban grid with square blocks from 300 to 350 feet long; a suburban field with rectangular blocks, 350-by-700 feet; and the larger agrarian hinterland of crop and pasture land, divided into half-mile squares, approximately 2640 feet in dimension, the result of the 160-acre "quarter" subdivisions of property that characterize this part of the midwestern United States. The Miller garden parcel, and the interior spatial subdivisions created by Kiley's bosques, lawns, and allées, reads as a spatial joint between these three fields with their varied dimensions and material properties [figure 4–23]. The garden can be understood as both the domestication of this agrarian plotting system and the regional scaling up of the city grid. From this geographical perspective, the spatial logic of the Miller house and garden represents its situation in new forms. It

/ **4-21** / *opposite*
DAN KILEY,
MILLER GARDEN,
COLUMBUS, INDIANA, 1955.
HOUSE AS INSIDE-OUT
LOGGIA.
/ WILLIAM MORRISH /
/ **4-22** / *right*
COLUMBUS, INDIANA,
AERIAL PHOTOGRAPH,
10 OCTOBER 1955.
/ USDA FARM SERVICE
AGENCY /

refers to regional landscapes, and transposes them into its boundaries, distilled and condensed.[62] The striated, overlapping bosques, hedges, clearings, and allées of its upper terrace, the focus of this article, are one-third of a ten-acre site that includes a meadow and wood within the Flatrock River floodplain, fifteen feet below. Garden, meadow, and grove, all part of the second nature of the Indiana rural landscape, are re-imagined and referenced, within the property [figure 4–24; see figure 4–9]. The Miller garden is both a modernist garden and a modern villa, abstract and engaged, detached and embedded, resonating with the syncopated rhythms of contemporary paintings such as Mondrian's 1942-43 *Broadway Boogie Woogie* and the agrarian landscape's alternating blocks of corn, soybeans, and wheat fields.[63]

While Kiley may have often been at odds with professional organizations such as the American Society of Landscape Architects (ASLA), his works are firmly within the traditions of the history of garden design. The Miller garden's multivalent references situate it not only within the spatial logics of modernism and the geography of Columbus and Bartholomew County, Indiana's land subdivision patterns [figure 4-23]. They connect us back to the essential role of gardens as spatial representations of their milieu. Here in a slightly longer excerpt from *Greater Perfections* John Dixon Hunt touches on the garden's dual obligation to being a space apart and yet connected:

> A garden will normally be out-of-doors, a relatively small space of ground (relative, usually, to accompanying buildings or topographical surroundings). The specific area of the garden will be deliberately related *through various means to the locality in which it is set: by the invocation of indigenous plant materials, by various modes of representation or other forms of reference (including association) to that larger territory, and by drawing out the character of its site (the genius loci).* The garden will thus be distinguished in various ways from the adjacent territories in which it is set. *Either it will have some precise boundary, or it will be set apart by the greater extent, scope, and variety of its design and internal organization; more usually, both will serve to designate its space and its actual or implied enclosure.*[64] [Emphases added]

A modernist landscape can also be a place related and yet distinguished from its adjacent territories. In fact, this aspect of the discipline of landscape architecture— site matters—should be part of any analysis of modern landscapes. Too many of the histories of this period bracket the projects too narrowly at the property line, missing other referents and meanings, as well as new interpretations, of the designed landscape.[65]

By considering Kiley's spatial principles in varied ways—as formal volumes, as embodied experiences, and as geographical representations—I have come to appreciate the spatiality of landscape modernism differently. While related to the spatial theories of modern art and architecture, it has medium-specific and canvas-specific characteristics. Unlike the modernist garden of Henry-Russell Hitchcock that is reduced to a terrace between a free plan house and nature, or of Joseph Hudnut that is a spatial extension from the house into the site, the Miller garden suggests a third approach.[66] Its garden spaces are related to both the spatial organization of a building and that of the larger context, but they are created with the unique properties

/ **4-23** /
SPATIAL FIELDS:
CITY, SUBURB, AND
COUNTRYSIDE. DETAIL OF
COLUMBUS, INDIANA,
AERIAL PHOTOGRAPH,
OCTOBER 10, 1955.
/ USDA FARM SERVICE
AGENCY /

of the landscape medium, and that matters; our reading vacillates between them as abstract art and situated geography, hybrid spaces with attributes of city, suburb, and countryside. Furthermore, the garden is lived, experienced through the moving body and known via the spatial practices of many bodies, over time.

/ CONCLUSIONS. SPATIAL CIRCUMSTANCES /

How did one project come to so embody American landscape modernism, and to crystallize several decades of spatial theorizing and testing? As I have suggested, for some decades prior to his commission, Kiley was part of a generation of landscape architects thinking about landscape modernism and the key role that spatial theory should have in the re-imagination of the designed landscape.[67] This intellectual history or context was coupled with several unique circumstances: Kiley had visited European gardens during and immediately after his military service in World War II and came to more fully appreciate the conceptual and perceptual aspects of landscape spatiality; his collaborator in the Miller garden was Eero Saarinen, whose father, Eliel, was one of several architects writing about the need for modern architects to consider space between buildings, the space of the landscape; and the actual site on the outskirts of Columbus, Indiana, the seam between city and country, imbued Kiley's emerging spatial principles and vocabulary with richer associations than might have existed in other projects.

Beyond the specific circumstances of the Miller garden and Columbus, Indiana, however, this inquiry into Kiley's prolonged absorption of diverse sources for his mature spatial principles and vocabulary holds lessons for designers as well as historians. Spatial theorizing, thinking, and making allowed Kiley to be expansive in his references and allusions, and to transcend the formal and informal stylistic categories that so vexed the profession for at least a half a century in America. Space was the mediating theory through which Kiley avoided, and transcended, dichotomies that plagued so many of his peers, such as classical and modern, high style and vernacular, or abstraction and placefulness. No wonder he prodded my friend, Anne, to instruct me, "make sure you will be talking in 3 dimensions when you get to him." Such a simple and concise preoccupation, space, opened up a world of invention and imagination to Kiley, and promises to do so for other landscape architects interested in making connections across categories, scales, geographies, and disciplines.

ACKNOWLEDGEMENTS

I owe considerable thanks to Reuben Rainey for his generous criticism and encouragement during the production of this essay, and former students Robin Lollar and Shanti Levy for their assistance and imagination with the analytical diagrams for the Miller garden. My colleague William Morrish generously shared his Miller garden slides with me, in addition to many more documents and slides that he assembled with Catherine Brown.

/ 4–24 /
DAN KILEY,
MILLER GARDEN,
COLUMBUS, INDIANA, 1955.
LAWN AND GROVE/MEADOW
AND WOODLOT.
SECOND NATURE REFERENCES
IN THE GARDEN.
/ WILLIAM MORRISH /

NOTES

1 This lecture evolved out of a paper written for a graduate seminar on modern architectural history taught by Richard G. Wilson. I developed that material into the Virginia AIA lecture, and then, with the encouragement of my professors Harry W. Porter and Reuben Rainey, into my first published article. See Elizabeth K. Meyer, "The Modern Framework," *Landscape Architecture*, 73 (March/April 1983), pp. 50–53.

2 This symposium, The Work of Dan Kiley: A Dialogue on Design Theory, took place on February 6, 1982, during my last semester of graduate school.

3 Kiley, "Panel Discussion," in Warren T. Byrd, Jr. and Reuben M. Rainey, eds., *The Work of Dan Kiley: A Dialogue on Design Theory* (Charlottesville, Va.: University of Virginia, School of Architecture, 1983), p. 29.

4 Gregg Bleam, "Modern and Classical Themes in the Work of Dan Kiley," in Marc Treib, ed., *Modern Landscape Architecture: A Critical Review* (Cambridge, Mass.: MIT Press, 1993); see essays by Anita Berrizbeitia, Dan Donovan, Gary Hilderbrand, and Mark Klopfer in William Saunders, ed., *Daniel Urban Kiley: The Early Gardens* (New York: Princeton Architecture Press, 1999); Gary Hilderbrand, *The Miller Garden: Icon of Modernism* (Washington, D.C.: Spacemaker Press,1999); Dan Kiley and Jane Amidon, *Dan Kiley: The Complete Works of America's Master Landscape Architect* (Boston: Bulfinch Press, 1999); Calvin Tomkins, "The Garden Artist," *New Yorker* (October 16, 1995), pp. 136–147; Peter Walker and Melanie Simo, *Invisible Gardens: The Search for Modernism in the American Landscape* (Cambridge, Mass.: MIT Press, 1994).

5 Kiley, "Lecture," *The Work of Dan Kiley*, p. 8.

6 See introduction by Joseph Disponsio, in Claude-Henri Watelet, *Essay on Gardens: A Chapter in the French Picturesque Translated into English for the First Time* (Philadelphia: University of Pennsylvania Press, 2003), and Sylvia Lavin, "Sacrifice and the Garden: Watelet's 'Essai sur les jardins' and the Space of the Picturesque," *Assemblage*, 28 (December 1995), pp. 16–33.

7 Adrian Forty, *Words and Buildings: A Vocabulary of Modern Architecture* (London: Thames and Hudson, 2000).

8 Frank Lloyd Wright, "In the Cause of Architecture IX: The Terms," *Architectural Record*, 64 (December 1928), p. 510.

9 Fletcher Steele, "New Pioneering in Garden Design," *Landscape Architecture*, 20 (April 1930), pp. 159–177.

10 Fletcher Steele, "Modern Garden Design," in Norman Taylor, ed., *The Garden Dictionary* (Boston: Houghton Mifflin, 1936), p. 505.

11 On numerous occasions Kiley remarked on Steele's influence on him and his classmates, James Rose and Garrett Eckbo. See Robin Karson, *Fletcher Steele* (New York: Harry H, Abrams, 1989), pp. 161, 335, for an account of the influence of Steele's writings on Kiley. Ten years later Kiley wrote, "We responded passionately...to Fletcher Steele's capacity to invest his designs with international influences." See Kiley and Amidon, *Dan Kiley: The Complete Works*, p. 11.

12 Siegfried Gideon, *Space, Time and Architecture: The Growth of A New Tradition* (Cambridge, Mass.: Harvard University Press, 1941).

13 Garrett Eckbo, Daniel U. Kiley, and James C. Rose, "Landscape Design in the Urban Environment," *Architectural Record* (May 1939), p. 81.

14 Ibid.

15 Anita Berrizbeitia, "Early Housing Projects and Garden Prototypes, 1941–52," in Saunders, *Kiley: The Early Gardens*, pp. 21–26.

16 Eckbo, Kiley, and Rose, "Landscape Design in the Urban Environment," p. 82.

17 See Saunders, Kiley: *The Early Gardens*, p. 80, for Joseph Disponsio's bibliographic notes on Kiley writing and scholarship.

18 See Bleam "Modern and Classical Themes in the Work of Dan Kiley," in Treib, *Modern Landscape Architecture*, p. 237, for a discussion of Mies van der Rohe's building plans and de Stijl spatial concepts.

19 See Henry-Russell Hitchcock and Philip Johnson, *The International Style: Architecture since 1922* (New York: Norton, 1932, 1966 reprint), pp. 48, 182–184, for plan and photographs.

20 This project was named Contempoville. See Marc Treib and Dorothée Imbert, *Garrett Eckbo: Modern Landscapes for Living* (Berkeley: University of California Press, 1997), pp. 110–113.

21 James Rose, "Freedom in the Garden," *Pencil Points*, 19 (October 1938), p. 640.

22 Aldred H. Barr, *Cubism and Abstract Art* (Cambridge, Mass: Belknap Press,

1986, reprint of 1936 catalog), pp. 156–157. Bleam, in "Modern and Classical Themes," notes this formal comparison, but does not appear to have reviewed the MOMA catalog directly. In the course of preparing this essay, I uncovered another book that explored this connection: Malene Hauxner, *Open to the Sky: The Second Phase of the Modern Breakthrough 1950–1970* (Copenhagen: Architektens Forlag and Danish Architectural Press, 2003), Section 2, "Space and Works: *Russian Dance*, J. Rose, G. Eckbo, D. Kiley and T. Church," pp. 90–111.

23 A typical example of this interpretation is Marc Treib, "Axioms for a Modernist Landscape," in Treib, *Modern Landscape Architecture*, p. 43.

24 Charles Downing Lay, "Space Composition," *Landscape Architecture*, 8 (January 1918), pp. 77–86.

25 Ibid., p. 86.

26 Ibid., pp. 78–79.

27 Steele, "New Pioneering in Garden Design" and "Modern Garden Design."

28 Lay, "Space Composition," p. 78.

29 Ibid., p. 83.

30 Adolf Hildebrand, *The Problem of Form in Painting and Sculpture* (New York: Stechert & Co, 1907), pp. 21, 28.

31 Reuben Rainey reminded me that Hubbard and Kimball's textbook, which was required reading at Harvard in the 1930s, has several sections on affect and mood in the landscape. These sections also drew on Santayana's aesthetic theories. See Henry V. Hubbard and Theodora Kimball, *An Introduction to the Study of Landscape Design* (New York: Macmillan Co, 1917, 1929, 1935).

32 Kiley, "Lecture," *The Work of Dan Kiley*, pp. 8–9.

33 Walker and Simo, *Invisible Gardens*, p. 186.

34 Kiley and Amidon, *Dan Kiley: The Complete Works*, p. 13.

35 Dan Kiley, "Nature: The Source of All Design," *Landscape Architecture* (January 1963), p. 127.

36 Erno Goldfinger "The Sensation of Space," *Architectural Review* (November 1941), pp. 129–131; and László Moholy-Nagy, *The New Vision* (New York: W.W. Norton & Co., 1938 rev. ed.).

37 Bruno Zevi, *Architecture as Space* (New York: Horizon Press, 1957), pp. 27, 32. See also Bruno Zevi, *Towards an Organic Architecture* (London: Faber & Faber, 1950), pp. 105–108, and 126, where he writes, "A unity of the interior and the garden: the garden as a projection of the interior space."

38 Erno Goldfinger, "Urbanism and Spatial Order," *Architectural Review* (December 1942), pp. 163–166. See his third article in this series, "The Elements of Enclosed Space," *Architectural Review* (January 1942), pp. 5–8.

39 Eliel Saarinen, *The City: Its Growth, Its Decay, Its Future* (Cambridge, Mass.: MIT Press, 1943), p. 52.

40 Joseph Hudnut, "The Modern Garden," in Christopher Tunnard, *Gardens in the Modern Landscape* (New York: Charles Scribner's, 1938; 1948 ed.), pp. 175–178.

41 Ibid., p. 178.

42 Zevi, *Architecture as Space*, p. 29.

43 Eckbo, Kiley, and Rose, "Landscape Design in the Urban Environment," p. 81. See also James Rose, *Creative Gardens* (New York: Reinhold, 1958), esp. "Definitions of Space," pp. 168–195, and "Plant Forms," pp. 196–203; and Margaret Olthof Goldsmith, *Designs for Outdoor Living* (New York: George W. Stewart, 1941).

44 Garrett Eckbo, "Outdoors and In: Gardens as Living Space" *Magazine of Art*, 34 (October 1941), p. 422.

45 Ibid., pp. 425–426.

46 James Rose, "Freedom in the Garden," *Pencil Points*, 19 (October 1938), p. 642.

47 James Rose, "Plants Dictate Garden Forms," *Pencil Points*, 19 (November 1938), p. 697.

48 Rose, *Creative Gardens*; and Goldsmith, *Designs for Outdoor Living*, pp. 343–349.

49 Kiley and Amidon, *Dan Kiley: The Complete Works*, p. 12.

50 In addition to the articles by Eckbo, Kiley, and Rose and others noted previously, there is one major text written in the same decades as the Miller garden that is explicit about landscape architecture as a spatial practice. See Garrett Eckbo, *Landscape for Living* (New York: F. W. Dodge Corp., 1950), "Space and People," and "From Art to Planning." The latter chapter is especially deserving of extended analysis for its discussion of "site-space planning," but this is outside the scope of this essay.

51 The diagrams in this essay were created by Shanti Fjord Levy and based on the January 23, 1958, revisions to the Irwin Miller Master Planting Plan (16 August 1957). I believe I was given this 27-by-30-inch blueprint by Anne Corcoran.

52 Elizabeth K. Meyer, "The Expanded Field of Landscape Architecture," in George Thompson and Frederick Steiner, eds., *Ecological Design and Planning* (New York: John Wiley, 1997), pp. 45–79.

53 Kiley and Amdion, *Dan Kiley: The Complete Works*, p. 25. Kiley also mentions the honey-locust allée in this account.

54 Michael Dirr, *Manual of Woody Landscape Plants* (Champaign, Ill.: Stipes, 1977), p. 250. This has been a classic reference book on plant characteristics and selection for several generations of designers.

55 John Dixon Hunt, *Greater Perfections: The Practice of Garden Theory* (Philadelphia: University of Pennsylvania Press, 2000), p. 15.

56 Felice Frankels's photographs are in Jory Johnson and Felice Frankel, *Modern Landscape Architecture: Redefining the Garden* (New York: Abbeville Press, 1991). Ezra Stoller's photographs are in an early article on the house, "A Contemporary Palladian Villa," *Architectural Forum*, 109 (September 1958), pp. 126–131. Alan Ward's photographs, taken between 1976 and 1996, are in several sources, including Hilderbrand, *The Miller Garden*, and Alan Ward, *American Designed Landscapes: A Photographic Interpretation* (Washington, D.C.: Spacemaker Press, 1996).

57 John Dixon Hunt, *The Afterlife of Gardens* (Philadelphia: University of Pennsylvania Press, 2004).

58 Rose, *Creative Gardens*, p. 170.

59 On November 18, 2008, a few months after Xenia Simons Miller's death, her family and the Indianapolis Museum of Art announced plans to create an endowment that will allow the museum to renovate the house, endow the maintenance of the house and garden, and to allow public access to both the house and garden (http://www.imamuseum.org/connect/currentnews. Viewed 2 January 2009).

60 Herbert Muschamp, "If Not Utopia, What Is It? The World by Kiley," *New York Times*, March 1, 1996.

61 Here, I am struck by Byrd and Rainey's insights captured in their introduction to the 1982 conference proceedings: "His art recalls the image of hedgerows and country roads, the meeting of the geometry of orchards with the natural roll of the land; it translates the sensation of passing through the deep shade of a sugar maple grove and bursting out upon a meadow. Consequently his design vocabulary is concerned less with individual plants and isolated things and more with the gathered momentum of fields and forests, a sustained line or lines in the landscape." Byrd and Rainey, *The Work of Dan Kiley*, p. 4.

62 See "The Idea of the Garden and the Three Natures," in Hunt, *Greater Perfections*, pp. 32-75. See Mirka Benes, "Pastoralism in the Roman Baroque Villa and in Claude Lorrain," in Mirka Benes and Dianne Harris, eds., *Villas in Early Modern Italy and France* (Cambridge, Mass.: Cambridge University Press, 2001), p. 103, for a definition of transposed sites, and the relationship between first and second nature, and the design of third nature, gardens.

63 The first article on the Miller House, "A Contemporary Palladian Villa," *Architectural Forum*, 109 (September 1958), pp. 126–131, focused on the building and architect, and referred to the project as a villa in comparison to Palladian architecture's facade and plan composition. Here I am thinking of the Miller Garden as a villa in the broader sense of the term—a country house within a matrix of gardens and groves, that is a place of cultural gatherings and individual retreat, with all the conveniences of the city.

64 Hunt, *Greater Perfections*, pp. 14–15.

65 See Elizabeth Meyer, "Site Citations: The Grounds of Modern Landscape Architecture," in Carol J. Burns and Andrea Kahn, eds., *Site Matters: Design Concepts, Histories, and Strategies* (New York: Routledge, 2005), pp. 93–130.

66 Henry-Russell Hitchcock, "Gardens in Relation to Modern Architecture," in *Contemporary Landscape Architecture and Its Sources*, exhibition catalog (San Francisco: San Francisco Museum of Art, 1937), pp. 13–19; and Joseph Hudnut, "The Modern Garden," in Tunnard, *Gardens in the Modern Landscape*.

67 See also essays in Saunders, *Kiley: The Early Gardens*.

Chronology

LISTED HERE ARE ONLY
THOSE MAJOR WORKS
DISCUSSED IN THIS BOOK.
ITS DATINGS ARE
INDEBTED TO;
DAN KILEY AND JANE AMIDON,
*DAN KILEY: THE COMPLETE
WORKS OF AMERICA'S MASTER
LANDSCAPE ARCHITECT*
(BOSTON: BULFINCH PRESS,
1999).

1939
Brief employent with the National Park Service

1939
Employed as an Associate Town Planner at the United
States Housing Authority in Washington, D.C., working
on low-income housing
Co-workers were Louis Kahn and Eero Saarinen

1939–1940
Co-author, with Garrett Eckbo and James Rose, of
a three-part manifesto on the practice of landscape
architecture published in *Architectural Record*

Completes his first major design project, the Charles
Collier estate in Falls Church, Virginia

1941
Opens the office of Dan Kiley in Washington, D.C., and
Franconia, New Hampshire

1942–1944
Military service in the U.S. Army Corps of Engineers

1944
Transferred to the Office of Strategic Services (OSS)

1945
Designs courtroom for the International War Crimes
Tribunal, Nuremburg, Germany

left
**FOUNTAIN PLACE,
DALLAS TEXAS, 1985.**
/ MARC TREIB /

right
**CURRIER FARM, DANBY,
VERMONT, 1959.**
/MARC TREIB /

1946–1951
Opens and maintains professional office in New
Hampshire and becomes a registered architect

1947
Jefferson National Expansion Memorial, St. Louis,
Missouri; architect: Eero Saarinen—constructed 1965

1951
Relocates professional office in Charlotte, Vermont,
near Lake Champlain: Dan Kiley and Partners

1955
Irwin and Xenia Miller garden, Columbus, Indiana;
architects: Eero Saarinen and Kevin Roche

1957–1968
United States Air Force Academy,
Colorado Springs, Colorado;
architect: Walter Netsch of Skidmore, Owings and Merrill

1958
Rockefeller University, New York, New York;
architect: Wallace Harrison

1960
Lincoln Center for the Performing Arts North Court,
New York, New York, with design team of Philip
Johnson, Eero Saarinen, Max Abramovitz, Wallace
Harrison, Gordon Bunshaft, and Pietro Belluschi

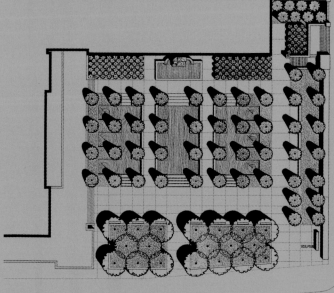

1962
Chicago Art Institute South Garden, Chicago, Illinois;
architect: Harry Weese

1963
Third Block of Independence Mall,
Philadelphia, Pennsylvania;
architects: Harbeson, Hough, Livingston and Larson

Dulles Airport, Chantilly, Virginia;
architect: Eero Saarinen

1964
Ford Foundation Building, New York, New York;
architects: Kevin Roche and John Dinkeloo

1965
Chicago Filtration Plant, Chicago, Illinois;
architects: C.F. Murphy Associates, Stanley Gladych

Clarence O. Hamilton garden, Columbus, Indiana;
architect: Anna Cabell Bliss

1969
Oakland Museum, Oakland, California;
associate landscape architect: Geraldine Knight Scott;
architects: Kevin Roche and John Dinkeloo

*From the mid-1960s to the mid-1970s the office
employed at times 35 individuals, including architects
and engineers.*

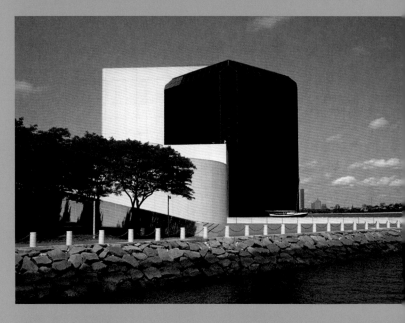

opposite bottom left
**THE KILEY OFFICE STAFF,
LAKE CHAMPLAIN,
VERMONT, 1967.**
/ OFFICE OF DAN KILEY /

opposite right above
**MILLER GARDEN,
COLUMBUS, INDIANA, 1955.**
/ MARC TREIB /

opposite right center
**ROCKEFELLER UNIVERSITY,
NEW YORK CITY, 1958.**
/ MARC TREIB /

opposite below
**SOUTH GARDEN,
ART INSTITUTE OF
CHICAGO, 1962. PLAN.**
/ FLL, HGSD /

right above
**JOHN F. KENNEDY LIBRARY,
BOSTON, MASSACHUSETTS,
1978.**
/ MARC TREIB /

right middle
**NCNB PLAZA,
TAMPA, FLORIDA, 1988.**
/ MARC TREIB /

right below
**KILEY HOUSE AND OFFICE,
CHARLOTTE, VERMONT.**
THE BOARDWALK
APPROACH.
/ MARC TREIB, 1991 /

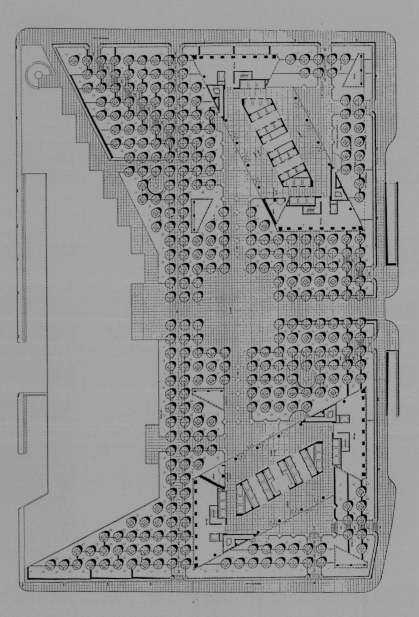

1974
Relocates office ten miles east of Charlotte, Vermont, and renames it Kiley/Tyndall/Walker

1977
National Gallery of Art East Wing, Washington, D.C.; architect: I. M. Pei

1978
Dalle Centrale, La Défense, Paris, France

John F. Kennedy Library, Boston, Massachusetts; architect: I.M. Pei

1979
Office renamed Dan Kiley/Peter Ker Walker

1983
Dallas Museum of Art, Dallas, Texas; architect: Edward Larabee Barnes

1985
Kiley decides to practice alone, with associates

Fountain Place, Dallas, Texas; architect: Harry Cobb, of Pei, Cobb, and Freed

1988
NCNB Plaza, Tampa, Florida [currently—2009—Bank of America Plaza]; architect: Harry Wolf

Henry Moore Sculpture Garden, Nelson-Atkins Museum of Art, Kansas City, Missouri; architect: Jaquelin Robertson

above
**HAMILTON GARDEN,
COLUMBUS, INDIANA, 1965.**
/ MARC TREIB /

middle
**UNITED STATES AIR FORCE
ACADEMY, COLORADO
SPRINGS, COLORADO, 1957–1968.**
/MARC TREIB /

below
**OAKLAND MUSEUM, OAKLAND,
CALIFORNIA, 1969.**
/ MARC TREIB /

opposite above
**FOUNTAIN PLACE,
DALLAS TEXAS, 1985.**
/ MARC TREIB /

opposite below
**FOUNTAIN PLACE, DALLAS
TEXAS. PLAN.**
/OFFICE OF DAN KILEY /

LEAR GARDEN, LOS ANGELES, CALIFORNIA, 1992.
/ MARC TREIB /

1990
The Getty Center, Los Angeles, California, architect: Richard Meier

Lear garden, Los Angeles, California

1996
Kimmel garden, Salisbury, Connecticut

While Kiley continued to design at a variety of scales, many of his commissions in the last decade of his practice were site plans for private residences.

2004
Dan Kiley dies at age 92

below
KIMMEL GARDEN, SALISBURY, CONNECTICUT, 1996.
/ MARC TREIB /

opposite
DAN KILEY AT HOME, CHARLOTTE, VERMONT, 1993.

/ KAREN MADSEN /

Contributors

John Beardsley is the Director of Garden and Landscape Studies at Dumbarton Oaks, Washington, D.C., and a Senior Lecturer in the Department of Landscape Architecture at the Harvard University Graduate School of Design. He is the author of numerous books on contemporary art and landscape design, including *Earthworks and Beyond: Contemporary Art in the Landscape* (1984); *Gardens of Revelation: Environments by Visionary Artists* (1995); and *Mario Schjetnan: Landscape, Architecture, and Urbanism* (2007). He has also organized many exhibitions, including The Quilts of Gees Bend, for the Museum of Fine Arts, Houston (2002), and Human/Nature: Art and Landscape in Charleston and the Low Country, for the Spoleto Festival USA in Charleston, S.C. (1997).

Gregg Bleam, founding principal of Gregg Bleam Landscape Architect in Charlottesville, Virginia, received his Masters of Landscape Architecture degree from Harvard University's Graduate School of Design where he has taught architecture and landscape design studios as well as at the University of Virginia. Before starting his own firm in 1990 he worked in the office of Dan Kiley in Vermont. His landscape designs have been recognized by the American Society of Landscape Architects and the American Institute of Architects. In 2005 he received an ASLA National Honor Award for his Garden of Planes project in Richmond, Virginia.

Elizabeth K. Meyer, FASLA, is a landscape architect and educator with interests in modern landscape architecture and contemporary design criticism. She has been on the faculty at the University of Virginia since 1993 and has served as department chair and graduate program director. Meyer's numerous publications have been included in anthologies such as *Ecological Design and Planning*, *Site Matters*, and *Large Parks*, and in numerous journals in the field. Her essay on Kiley's spatial practices is part of a book-in-progress called *Groundwork: Theory and Practices of Modern Landscape Architecture*. She is a frequently invited lecturer at universities and international conferences, and a jury member for national design competitions.

Reuben M. Rainey is William Stone Weedon Professor Emeritus in the School of Architecture of the University of Virginia and a former chair of the Department of Landscape Architecture. His research and publications cover a broad range of topics, including nineteenth- and twentieth-century park design, historic preservation, Italian Renaissance villas, the design of spaces in medical facilities, and the work of major twentieth-century American landscape architects. His most recent book is *Modern Public Gardens: The Suburban Parks of Robert Royston*, co-authored with JC Miller. He also is executive producer of *GardenStory*, a ten-part documentary for public television focusing on the ways gardens transform the lives of individuals and their communities

Marc Treib, Professor of Architecture Emeritus at the University of California, Berkeley, has held Fulbright, Guggenheim, and Japan Foundation fellowships, as well as an advanced design fellowship at the American Academy in Rome. A noted landscape and architectural historian and critic, he has published widely on modern and historical subjects in the United States, Japan, and Scandinavia. Recent books include: *Noguchi in Paris: The Unesco Garden* (2003); *Thomas Church, Landscape Architect: Designing a Modern California Landscape* (2004); *The Donnell and Eckbo Gardens: Modern California Masterworks* (2005); *Settings and Stray Paths: Writings on Landscapes and Gardens* (2005); *Representing Landscape Architecture* (2007); and *Drawing/Thinking: Confronting an Electronic Age* (2008).

Acknowledgements

Several individuals have been immensely helpful in the realization of this project. Richard E. Wolfe suggested it as a result of his auditing courses in the history of landscape architecture at the University of Virginia. Molly and Richard Wolfe, Karin and Mark Ohrstrom, Arlene and Charles Semel, Sheila Wolk, Imogene and Andrew Ruppel, and Charles Matheson most generously funded the entire project. Madelyn Wessel, Special Advisor to the University of Virginia Librarian, was most helpful in resolving legal issues involved. Sue Rainey's careful and insightful editing was indispensable. Mary Daniels, Librarian, Special Collections, the Frances Loeb Library, Harvard Graduate School of Design, called to my attention and helped provide several valuable illustrations of Dan Kiley's work. Marc Treib created a masterful design for the book and offered valuable critical advice as co-editor. Alan Ward and Aaron Kiley were most generous in sharing their stunning photographs of several of Kiley's projects, and William Morrish provided key images of the Miller house and garden from his personal collection. William Stout offered encouragement throughout the project and oversaw the production of the book with his usual high standards of professionalism. Gregg Bleam generously consented to the reprint of his essay on Kiley, and John Beardsley and Elizabeth K. Meyer took time from their extremely busy schedules to contribute new essays. Graduates of the School of Architecture of the University of Virginia, Liza Mueller, Mary Williams, Helen Wilson, Bradford Bellows, Robin Lollar, and Shanti Levy helped create insightful analytical drawings for the essays by Gregg Bleam and Elizabeth K. Meyer. And, finally, Dean Karen Van Lengen of the University of Virginia School of Architecture granted permission for the re-issuing of the symposium publication and provided valuable advice on the project throughout its development.

Reuben M. Rainey
William Stone Weedon Professor Emeritus
School of Architecture
University of Virginia

Index